Starting Out AND Being Successful IN Commercial Real Estate

By JM Padron

ISBN: 978-1-62550-564-4 (PB)

       978-1-62550-565-1 (EB)

Library of Congress Control Number: 2018912362

Acknowledgements

I would like to thank my wife and children in special Helen who worked with me for the last 10 years.

Additionally I would like to thank Carolyn Weber, Ricardo Cardenas, Sergio Felgueres Sr. and Sergio Felgueres Jr. for opening my eyes in this education, training and coaching Endeavour.

Prologue

Welcome to the wonderful world of commercial real estate! Perhaps you purchased this book because you are a residential agent who always wanted to "do a commercial deal" or perhaps shift your focus to commercial properties and clients. Maybe you're new to the world of commercial real estate and you want to ensure you grasp the fundamentals, as you recognize these are essential to launching your career. Or maybe you are already a seasoned commercial real estate veteran, and as a lifetime learner you continue to work on improving your skills.

Regardless of why you selected this book, you want to learn. As the founder of the Massimo Group, North America's premier commercial real estate coaching organization, I have had the privilege of working with scores of top producing brokers, and most talented coaches, such as JM Padron, in the world. They too are lifelong learners.

Starting Out and Being Successful in Commercial Real Estate will introduce you to 3 essential elements of commercial real estate brokerage success:

- Identify the different types of properties and understand the difference between an end user and investor.

- Understand the fundamentals of financial analysis and the performance of an investment, including financing leverage and how to estimate value.

- Recognize the difference of working with buyers/tenants and owners/landlords, how to master an exclusive listing presentation and procuring an exclusive buyer/tenant representation agreement.

Whether *Starting Out and Being Successful in Commercial Real Estate* serves as your launching pad or a refresher, it will provide you with the information you need to grow your commercial real estate skills. JM's book provides you a guide to be better prepared for the complex, crazy and wonderful world of commercial real estate.

Rod N. Santomassimo, CCIM
Founder / CEO
The Massimo Group

Starting Out in Commercial Real Estate

Realtors aren't allowed to sell commercial, right?

If you are already a Broker or licensed Salesperson, you know for a fact that you can transact different property types: Condos, Single Family Homes, Luxury and Duplexes. Some agents sell/lease them all; and some others specialize in a particular type, such as the Luxury Market.

The real estate license allows agents legally practice commercial real estate even though they do not possess the competency. However the National Association of Realtors (NAR) code of ethics, presents very clear in Article 11:

"Article 11.

*The services which REALTORS® provide to their clients and customers shall conform to the standards of **practice** and **competence** which are reasonably expected in the specific real estate disciplines in which they engage; specifically, residential real estate brokerage, real property management, **commercial** and **industrial** real estate brokerage, land brokerage, real estate appraisal, real estate counseling, real estate syndication, real estate auction, and international real estate.*

REALTORS® shall not undertake to provide specialized professional services concerning a type of property or service that is outside their field of competence unless they engage the assistance of one who is competent on such types of property or service, or unless the facts are fully disclosed to the client. Any persons engaged to provide such assistance shall be so identified to the client and their contribution to the assignment should be set forth."

Therefore, a real estate license must acquire the competence or engage the assistance of one who is competent in the commercial real estate field or must disclosed the client that the commercial real estate practice is outside their scope of business.

I do not intent to make real estate agents competent after reading my book, what I do pretend is to make them open their eyes and understand what the commercial real estate field comprehends. Reading this book will bring the necessary knowledge to understand the language of the industry, and the concepts and terms involved in practicing commercial real estate.

It is an excellent tool to understand the commercial real estate business and to be able to either refer good business or partner with a seasoned commercial practitioner. If the agent chooses the path of entering into the world of commercial real estate, these are my recommendations:

1. Partner with an experienced commercial broker.

2. Take a basic commercial real estate course, including financial concepts and calculations as well as the process to estimate value, leasing, working with buyers, working with sellers and the process of due diligence. I have designed a 4 day class that covers all these topics, called CCP, Certified Commercial Practitioner.

3. Take at least two classes of the CCIM program: CE-101 "Financial Analysis for Commercial Investment Real Estate" and CE-102 "Market Analysis for Commercial Investment Real Estate". My advice is to complete the program as follows:

The CCIM Program:

Every candidate for the CCIM designation is required to complete an education component, pass the Comprehensive Exam, complete a membership application, and pay annual dues. All candidates except Fast Track members will also have to submit a Portfolio of Qualifying Experience for review.

How to Succeed in Commercial Real Estate

Contents

Introduction to Commercial Real Estate

Introduction

As in other professions, succeeding in commercial real estate requires that you be able to speak the language of the industry. Some residential agents start practicing commercial real estate without the basic knowledge, making it a difficult uphill climb. Residential agents can learn the hard way through experience, but this is a waste of precious time, which might have been used to close deals. I remember when I stated practicing real estate some years back, I began as a residential agent in a residential franchise office. My goal since the beginning was to transition to the commercial practice. Soon, I realized that, without the proper education and experience, the path is too steep, nearly 90-degrees straight up. I remember calling commercial brokers to find out about their listings, and after just a few words, they would complain about the competence of practicing real estate agents, and usually, hang up on me. This situation was frustrating and I understood that it wouldn't be easy to transition to commercial real estate. That's when I started looking for the right path. I met with some commercial agents, who were kind enough to give me some hints on how to start this difficult journey. And guess what? Most of them agreed that getting the proper education was the first step. Just a few of them, whom I later found had learned the business the hard way, recommended that I start working as an assistant to a seasoned commercial broker. The truth is, success is a combination of education and experience, but having the right education up front accelerates the process of getting that experience.

The first step is to understand the key terms and concepts in commercial real estate and familiarize yourself with the language and definitions used in this field.

In this section, we will cover the concepts and definitions used in day-to-day practice as well as looking into common situations you may encounter in this arena.

Just as in my case, most commercial real estate professionals begin as residential agents, then transition to commercial real estate. Therefore, it is useful to identify the main differences between the two fields.

Realtors aren't allowed to sell commercial, right?

If you are already a Broker or licensed Salesperson, you know for a fact that you can handle transactions for different property types: Condos, Single Family Homes, Luxury residences, and Duplexes. Some agents sell/lease them all; and others specialize in a particular type, such as the Luxury Market.

A real estate license allows agents to legally practice commercial real estate even though they do not possess the competency. However, the National Association of Realtors (NAR) code of ethics, presents the case very clearly in Article 11:

> *"Article 11.*
>
> *The services which REALTORS® provide to their clients and customers shall conform to the standards of **practice** and **competence,** which are reasonably expected in the specific real estate disciplines in which they engage; specifically, residential real estate brokerage, real property management, **commercial** and **industrial** real estate brokerage, land brokerage, real estate appraisal, real estate counseling, real estate syndication, real estate auction, and international real estate.*
>
> *REALTORS® shall not undertake to provide specialized professional services concerning a type of property or service that is outside their field of competence unless they engage the assistance of one who is competent on such types of property or service, or unless the facts are fully disclosed to the client. Any persons engaged to provide such assistance shall be so identified to the client and their contribution to the assignment should be set forth."*

Therefore, a real estate licensee must acquire the necessary competence or engage the assistance of one who is competent in the commercial real estate field or must disclose to the client that commercial real estate practice is outside their scope of business.

I do not intend to make real estate agents competent after reading my book. What I do intend is to make them open their eyes and understand what the commercial real estate field is all about. This book will provide understanding of the language of the industry, along with the concepts and terms involved in practicing commercial real estate.

It's an excellent tool that will help you understand the commercial real estate business and enable you to either refer good business or partner with a seasoned commercial practitioner. If you, the agent, choose to enter into the world of commercial real estate, these are my recommendations:

1. Partner with an experienced commercial agent.

2. Take a basic commercial real estate course, including financial concepts and calculations and learn about estimating value, leasing, working with buyers, working with sellers, and the process of due diligence. I have designed a 4-day class that covers all these topics, called CCP, Certified Commercial Practitioner.

3. Take at least two classes of the CCIM program: CE-101 "Financial Analysis for Commercial Investment Real Estate" and CE-102 "Market Analysis for Commercial Investment Real Estate." My advice is to complete the program as follows:

The CCIM Program:

Every candidate for the CCIM designation is required to complete an education component, pass the Comprehensive Exam, complete a membership application, and pay annual dues. All candidates, except Fast Track members, will also have to submit a Portfolio of Qualifying Experience for review.

Education Component

The education component of earning your CCIM designation is comprised of a four-course curriculum, an online ethics course, negotiation training, and elective courses from the Ward Center for Real Estate Studies:

CI 101: Financial Analysis for Commercial Investment Real Estate. This course is a prerequisite for CI 102-CI 104 and will provide you with the foundation of practical financial analysis skills you need to succeed in the following courses and in the field.

CI 102: Market Analysis for Commercial Investment Real Estate
Analyze investment factors for each of four major property types: office, industrial, multifamily, and retail.

Negotiation Training

Eight hours of training on the CCIM Interest-Based Negotiations Model is required before going on to CI 103 and CI 104. This requirement can be completed through the online Preparing to Negotiate course, the one-day classroom course, Commercial Real Estate Negotiations, or the two-day classroom Advanced Negotiation Workshop.

CI 103: User Decision Analysis for Commercial Investment Real Estate
Use market and financial analysis skills for user space decisions, and apply cost-of-occupancy models for ownership and leasing.

CI 104: Investment Analysis for Commercial Investment Real Estate
Optimize investment returns and effectively forecast investment performance by quantifying real estate risk.

Online Ethics Course

This free training covers the CCIM Code and Standards of Practice of CCIM Institute.

Portfolio of Qualifying Experience

To demonstrate their experience in commercial real estate, candidates must submit a portfolio of qualifying activities, transactions, projects, or work products. This portfolio can take one of three forms, depending on your level of experience and the type of work that will be included.

Transactional portfolios must meet minimum volume requirements:

Three (3) or more qualifying activities totaling $30 million or more; or

Exactly ten (10) qualifying activities totaling $10 million or more; or

Twenty (20) qualifying activities with no dollar volume requirement.

Comprehensive Exam

The Comprehensive Exam is a full-day exam testing your mastery of the concepts introduced in the core CCIM courses. It's preceded by the two-day Course Concepts Review, allowing candidates the opportunity to review the key topics that will be covered on the exam.

If you need further information, go to www.ccim.com

As we can see becoming an expert in commercial real estate requires a lot of learning, accumulated experience, and good negotiations skills.

Commercial Real Estate Vs Residential Real Estate

Comparing commercial real estate to residential real estate is like comparing apples to oranges; both are fruit, but that is where the similarities end.

Commercial real estate has to do with business and rates of return; residential real estate deals with emotions.

Residential real estate revolves around the wants and needs of a homeowner and his family. It involves property purchased for individual use, most often to provide housing. People buy houses and condos to live in, to make that particular property their home. They deal with variables such as quality and proximity of schools, space layout to accommodate their furniture, relaxing spaces such as a pool deck, etc.

In residential real estate, decisions are made by heart; it is not about analyzing whether or not that property will generate income.

Commercial Property

Residential Property

The following are general descriptions of the two types of real estate:

Commercial real estate is business-focused. It involves property that is sold, leased, or used to achieve a predetermined business objective. It is used as an investment to achieve an anticipated rate of return on the funds invested, therefore creating wealth.

The selling process for commercial real estate is based on numbers and financial calculations. The key factor is the return on investment, how much money must be put down to get a desired return.

Residential real estate is more likely to involve an emotional purchase. Even though residential buyers look at the comparable sold homes in the market before deciding to buy, many buyers make decisions because the house just feels right to them. The key factor is to satisfy the physiological needs of the buyer and his or her family. The first priority is not about expecting a return on investment.

Dealing with commercial real estate is very different than working with residential real estate. In residential real estate, you deal with single family homes, duplexes, and apartments or condos. Usually, you perform CMAs to determine the value of the properties. In commercial real estate, you deal with office buildings, retail stores, warehouses, and more, and you perform financial analyses, market analyses and BPOs including all three of these methods to determine value: Sales Comparable Approach, Cost Reposition Approach, and Income Approach.

A few basic issues to consider involving commercial real estate.

What is included in the commercial real estate properties?

You may not always be clear on whether a property is commercial or residential. Defining what is and what is not commercial real estate can be challenging. There are, of course, obvious examples of commercial real estate in all parts of the world such as, for example, an office downtown, a shopping center, or a warehouse.

What about an industrial property downtown that has been converted into ten apartment units?

As a factory, it was obviously a commercial property. However, now that it is for residential use, would it be considered residential?

In the United States, commercial properties are those that have five dwelling units or more. This definition is limited by law in the United States, but depending on the zoning and the laws of each site, you might find different nuances.

The apartment building that started as a warehouse might very well be a residential property if, for example, the owner has assigned five apartments to each member of his family and sold the remaining units to friends and acquaintances as a mini-condo project.

Now what about if the 10 apartments are rented out to generate monthly income?

This would then be considered a multifamily property falling within commercial real estate categories.

A successful real estate professional is knowledgeable about product types, user and investor needs, and the markets in which the participants and properties interact. This knowledge of product, user, and investor needs in specific markets is critical to successfully serving both clients and customers.

There are two primary components in the commercial real estate world: physical, improved properties or land to be developed (improved). Buyers may acquire properties for operating businesses, generating income and appreciation, or for both.

There are two patterns in the relationship between people and property. On the one hand, Users/Tenants and on the other, Investors/Landlords. Users/Tenants use space to operate a business; Investors/Landlords expect other people to use their space and their aim is the income the space will generate, and its appreciation over time to accumulate wealth.

There are two types of clients a commercial real estate professional may represent: End Users and Investors.

End Users:

End users may be buyers or tenants who make decisions regarding space that they need to use for running their business. i.e. A retail space used for a drycleaner.

Investors:

Investors analyze the feasibility of investment in properties that are or could be leased to others, or land that could be developed, or which will appreciate over time. Both sellers and buyers are included in this category. i.e. Investment in a shopping center with multiple tenants.

Tenants rent space from owners of commercial real estate, they make decisions to rent or to buy. Tenant/buyers analyze different scenarios, based on: the premises layout and size, the product they sell, the demographics, driving times, traffic counts, and access/egress facilities. Additionally, and probably the most important analysis is the financial performance of the space when compared with their cost of money. The commercial real estate professional must understand and handle all these concepts to be able to properly provide wise advice to his or her clients.

Investors are individuals or companies that acquire commercial properties as a commodity that can generate cash flow and appreciate over time to accumulate wealth. Investors buy properties that tenants rent, based on cash flow projected for the "holding period" at a desired rate of return.

Investors look for what I call the triple play of an investment.

1. Yearly increase of the rental income.
2. Yearly appreciation of the property.
3. Amortization to principal, thus creating equity.

It is of crucial importance to know and to understand the motivations and risk tolerance of the investor. Users and investors are continuously bombarded with tons of information about the market and the roles that different factors play in the transaction. It is our responsibility to guide them in how to use this information to their benefit by explaining to them the weight of each.

Each market has its own separate characteristics, and each must be defined clearly so we can understand how it interacts with the others.

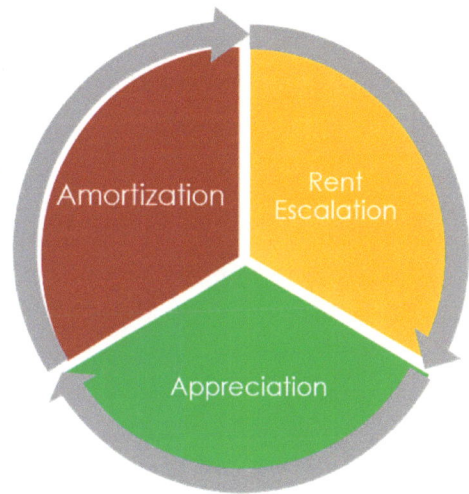

Types of Real Estate Markets

People frequently ask the famous question: "How is the market?" The correct answer to which is, "It depends." Many factors may be involved. Are we talking about the market for office buildings? The Miami market or New York Are you buying or renting? The type of market must be specifically defined.

There are two main categories to consider when defining the market:

The Physical Market

This is an existing space in a determined geographic area. The availability of space is determined by the vacancy and absorption rates. In other words by supply and demand. Demographics, regulations concerning issues such as land use and permitting and use determine the availability of space in a determined period of time. If demand for retail space increases and supply decreases, we say

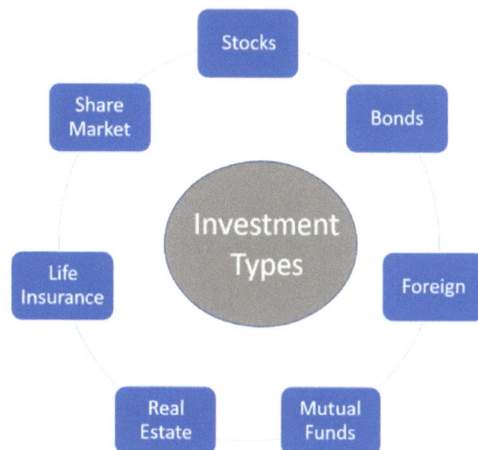

that we are in a landlords' market and rents tend to increase. On the other hand, if developers have overbuilt retail space, rents will tend to decrease, and we will be in a tenant's market. The ideal scenario is to take into consideration all the relevant economic factors to achieve a stable market picture.

Real Estate Investment

Real estate competes with other investments including stocks and bonds, and most importantly, the investor's cost of money. Why would an investor buy a commercial property which results in an ROI below the desired rate? Investors must analyze in detail the risk, the cost to borrow capital, the leverage, and the cash requirements involved. The amount of cash the investor puts into the transaction is called equity.

The combination of the space and investment markets, determines the absorption rate, therefore the feasibility of new construction. The interaction of these two markets will also determine rents and trends as well as the market value of each property. The estimated market value of commercial properties will be covered later in this book.

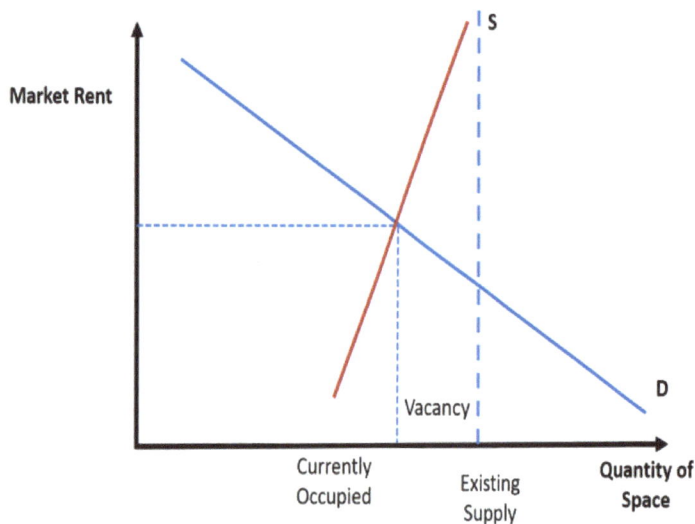

Geography and Types of Properties

To be successful in commercial real estate, it is very important to understand the specific property types and the geographic markets they are in. It is important to specialize in one or more of each type of property, because even though they all generate wealth, their performance varies from type to type. Even within one category, we find specialization in sub-categories. For instance, a commercial broker may like Industrial, but because of his location, he may specialize in industrial flex space. Likewise, another broker may like retail, but may specialize in Single Tenant NNN properties.

Within any commercial real estate market, it is also important to understand the architectural and use trends for specific property types. For example, in the office market, tenants may look for "smart buildings" and amenities such as restaurant, terrace, and gym facilities.

Demographics, as mentioned before, are also important, probably the most important factor to take into consideration when working a specific geographic area: labor force, expenditure partners, population mix, etc.

As stated above, specializing is a key point in the practice of commercial real estate but we must be aware of the geography or size of the market in which we operate. In the small markets, a commercial practitioner must become a multi property specialist, because of the scarce inventory available in one specific category of property.

Classification of Commercial Property

Commercial Real Estate is divided into the following eight categories:

1. Office Buildings
2. Industrial
3. Retail
4. Multifamily Housing
5. Hospitality
6. Special Purpose
7. Developable Land
8. Business Opportunities, "Going Concern"

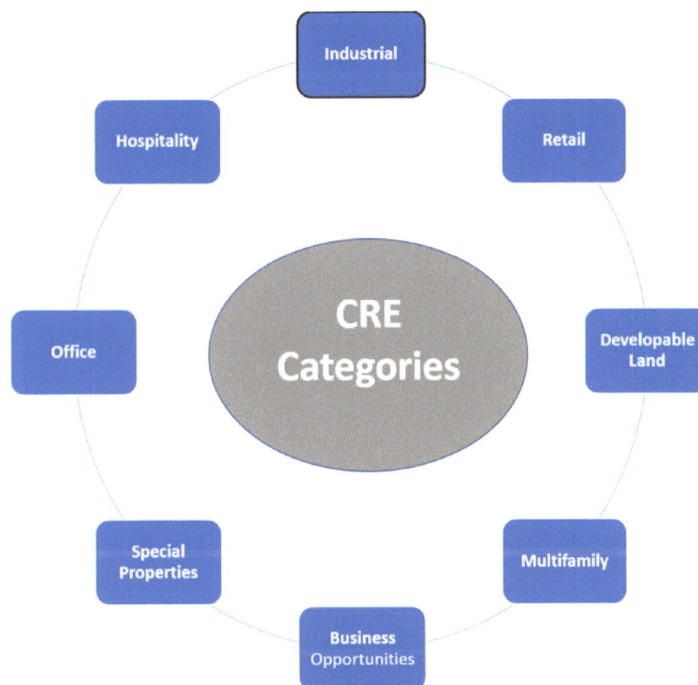

At the same time these eight categories are subdivided into sub-classifications, such as:

- Government buildings, medical office buildings, educational buildings, etc.
- Factories, Warehouses, Distribution Centers, Research and Development Centers.
- Shopping Centers, Supermarkets, Shops, Restaurants, etc.
- Garden Buildings, Mid Height Buildings, Tall Buildings, Buildings with Facilities, etc.
- Motels, Hotels, Resorts, etc.
- Marinas, Cemeteries, Ranches, Theme Parks, Golf Courses, etc.
- Lots to Urbanize, Lots for Industrial Developments, Lots for Mixed Developments, etc.
- Sandwich Shop, Mobil phone store, Hardware Stores, Manufacturing facilities.

People tend to associate commercial real estate properties with office buildings, shopping centers and business parks; however, it should be noted that land, depending on its use, can be considered as commercial real estate as well.

A "going concern" is a company that has the resources to continue to operate for the foreseeable future. Business transactions may or may not include the improved property. For example, a restaurant can be sold as a going concern and may or may not include ownership of the building in which it operates.

A going concern is also known as a business opportunity. When I started practicing commercial real estate after having learned the basics and working out some deals, I saw that most of the residential agents out there thought of commercial real estate only as business opportunities I used to hear things like, "Oh that's a great business; you always make 10% commission," But business opportunities is only one category in commercial practice.

Moving on, we will now define the different categories in commercial real estate. It is important to understand that these different classifications are standardized, but the commercial practitioner must adapt these definitions to his market place. For instance, a high-rise office building in New York City may be in the same category as one in a suburb like Weston, FL where I practice real estate, but they may be different by orders of magnitude. Hence, there are sub-categories that are also relevant.

Office Buildings

Office buildings can be sub-categorized by their height and their quality. It is important to mention that these classifications are standard but they will vary from market to market. To cite an example, it is not the same to consider an office building in Manhattan the same as an office building in Albany, where only the Erastus Corning Tower and the Alfred E. Smith State Office Building may be considered as high-rises since they have 44 and 34 stories respectively. The commercial broker should use this as a pattern to define the classifications in his own market.

Based on Height, office buildings are classified as:

Low Rise: usually fewer than 7 floors above the ground level

Mid Rise: between 7 and 25 floors above the ground level

High Rise: more than 25 floors above ground level

Low-Rise   Mid-Rise   High-Rise

Based on the quality, office buildings are classified as:

Class A Buildings: These properties typically have high-quality standards, using exceptional finishes, ease of access, modern designs, and smart technology. Class A buildings may also provide amenities such as cafeterias, fitness centers, and reception services, along with monitoring, valet parking, etc.

These buildings fetch the highest base rents and additional rents in the market.

Class B buildings: These properties present moderate finishes, small or no reception, and do not have the types of amenities provided by class A buildings. Class B buildings generate lower rents than class A buildings. Class B buildings can be brand new constructions or recently renovated structures.

Class C buildings: These properties have outmoded finishes and most of them present a certain degree of obsolescence. Class C buildings generate lower rents than class B buildings.

Industrial

Bulk Warehouse: These represent the simplest of all the industrial spaces, being conformed by no more than four walls, a roof and a floor. Properties of this type can be very large, with an average of 50,000 square feet (SF) as a minimum. These properties have ample clear spans and very high ceilings. Rents may be priced per cubic foot.

Office Warehouse: This category of industrial space may devote 5 to 25 percent of its space to office requirements and typically is constructed of metal, brick, block, or wood. This category typically features loading docks and is located near or within city limits. Good highway access is an important consideration for office/warehouse properties.

Office/Service: These properties tend to be more expensive buildings located in attractive, park-like settings with landscaping. They are usually at the highest end of market rents and devote more than 25 percent of their space to offices. Office/service properties are similar to research and development facilities. They typically are located along major arteries.

Research and Development: This category is a hybrid of office and manufacturing. The research and development category is the most people-intensive of industrial properties and requires the highest parking ratios. Tenants of these properties usually require many improvements, such as "clean rooms" for integrated circuit manufacturing, laboratories, cafeterias, lounges, and other amenities. Among commercial properties, research and development properties have rental and sale values second only to "pure" office space. They often are located near universities and a white-collar labor base.

Free Standing: This category often is developed in an industrial park setting or erected as a build-to-suit on a selected piece of property. Freestanding properties usually are designed for manufacturing, distribution, assembly, packaging, and similar uses. These properties vary in their construction types, design, ceiling height, utility services, amount of land, and usually are designed, built and occupied by an owner/user for a special purpose

Multi-Tenant: This type of industrial property attracts the smallest user of industrial space (1,000 to 5,000 sf). It is often situated in a complex of similar buildings, where necessary support services are in or near the complex. Multi-tenant properties might contain incubator space for start-up high tech, warehousing, or distribution tenants renting on a short-term basis. Buildings for such tenants usually require 18-foot or higher ceilings, efficient truck-loading arrangements, and space for offices.

Large Manufacturing: These facilities are used for manufacturing, production, assembly, shipping and receiving, or major production processes. Size is based on the user's requirements. These properties are often radically modified to suit a particular product or process, and therefore are prone to functional obsolescence.

Industrial Parks: This is a planned development often controlled and managed by a person or investment entity as a fund for a real estate investment trust (REIT). The types and nature of usages are controlled in order to protect and preserve compatibility. Industrial parks can serve as mixed-use, single use, special uses, scientific and technological, or for complex communications systems.

Shopping Centers/Retail

Strip Center: These are strips of commercially zoned land divided into parcels to be developed for retail use. They usually have a narrow trade area and offer a variety of services such as a convenience store, a barber shop, a sandwich shop, etc. The tenants of these type of centers are called "Ma and Pa," a colloquial term for a small, independent, family-owned business. Unlike franchises and large corporations, which have multiple operations in various locations, Ma and Pa shops usually have a single location that often occupies a physically small space.

Neighborhood Center: This center is designed to provide convenient shopping for the day-to-day needs of consumers in the immediate vicinity. According to the publication of the International Council of Shopping Centers ("ICSC"), the majority are anchored by supermarkets, while close to a third offer a pharmacy as the anchor. A neighborhood center in general, is configured as an "L" shape. It accommodates shoppers in the immediate neighborhood for convenience items, such as laundry, hair and nail care, tanning salons, mail and package stores, and gift items.

Community Center: This is a shopping center of approximately 100,000 to 300,000 square feet and 20 to 70 retail spaces, designed for a mixture of retailers and food service establishments with a high convenience factor for a market area radius of 3 to 6 miles. Usually situated on 10 to 40 acres, with at least one anchor tenant, which typically uses 40 to 60 percent of the gross leasable space. The community center usually offers a wide range of clothing and other products in addition to what is provided in a neighborhood center. Among the most common anchors are supermarkets, super-pharmacies, and large discount stores. In the Community Center, tenants sell items such as clothing, household, furniture, toys, electronic products, and/or sporting goods.

Free Standing: This is a commercial establishment providing goods and services in single- or multiple-use buildings of various sizes. The larger, newer freestanding stores also are referred to as "big boxes." These improved properties are suitable for lease-back transactions. Usually, drugstores, department stores, automotive stores, toy stores fall in this category. Most of these retailers, based on their cost of money, acquire the land and build the facilities. Once the store is opened and stabilized, they lease it back to an investor.

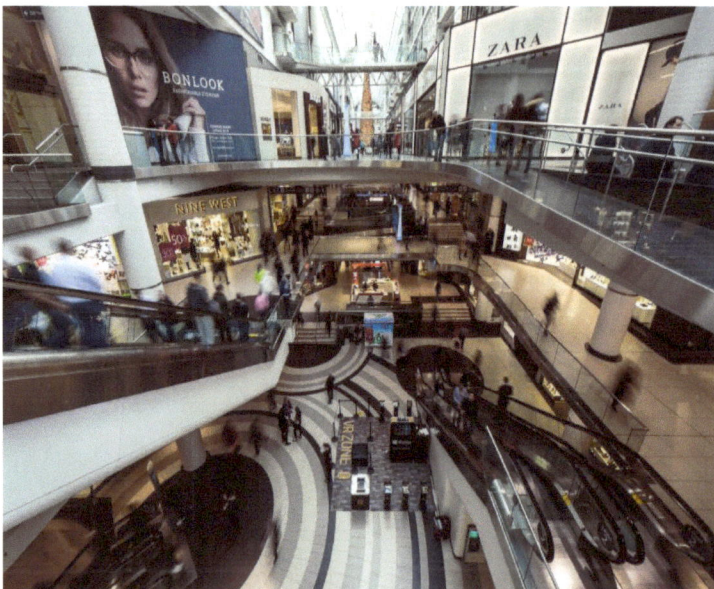

Regional Center: This is a large shopping center that draws customers from outside the part of town in which it is located. According to the International Council of Shopping Centers, it is one offering general merchandise, with 400,000 to 800,000 square feet of space sitting on 40 to 100 acres with two or more anchor tenants taking up 50 to 70 percent of the available space. The typical market area is a radius of 5 to 15 miles, or approximately 80 to 700 square miles. This type of center offers goods in general, a large percentage of which is provided by the garment industry, and services throughout the whole range and variety. Its main attractions are its anchors: traditional, mass market, discount department stores to specialty of fashion. A typical regional center is usually surrounded with an orientation toward the interior of the establishments connected by a shared corridor with parking at the perimeter.

Super Regional Center: A super regional center is, per the International Council of Shopping Centers in the US, a shopping mall with over 800,000 sq. ft. (74,000 m2) of gross leasable area, three or more anchors, mass merchants, more variety, fashion apparel, etc., serving as the dominant shopping venue for the region (within 25 miles or 40 km) in which it is located. Similar to the regional center, but larger in size, a super-regional center has a wider selection of merchandise, and is based on a greater population base. As with the regional centers, the typical configuration is as an enclosed mall, often with multiple levels.

Power Center: A large (250,000 to 750,000 square ft.) outdoor shopping center which usually includes three or more "big box" stores, as well as smaller retailers and restaurants (either free-standing or located in strip plazas), surrounded by a shared parking lot. Power centers are built for the convenience of motorists. Unlike traditional big box stores, power centers often have distinctive architectural features. This type of center is dominated by large retailers, including discount department stores, off-price stores, and warehouse clubs, or "category killers." Category killers are stores that offer tremendous selection in a particular merchandise category at low prices such as shoes, pet supplies, or sporting goods.

Fashion Specialty Center: This type of center is composed mainly of upscale apparel shops, boutiques, and craft shops carrying selected fashion or unique merchandise of high quality and price. These centers need not be anchored, although sometimes restaurants or entertainment can provide an alternative to high-profile anchors. The physical design of the center is sophisticated, emphasizing a rich décor and high-quality landscaping. These centers are usually found in trade areas with high income levels.

Theme/Festival Center: These centers typically employ a unifying theme that is carried out by the individual shops in their architectural design and, to an extent, in their merchandise. The biggest appeal of these centers is to tourists; restaurants and entertainment facilities can anchor them. These centers, generally located in urban areas, tend to be adapted from older, sometimes historic, buildings and can be part of mixed-use projects.

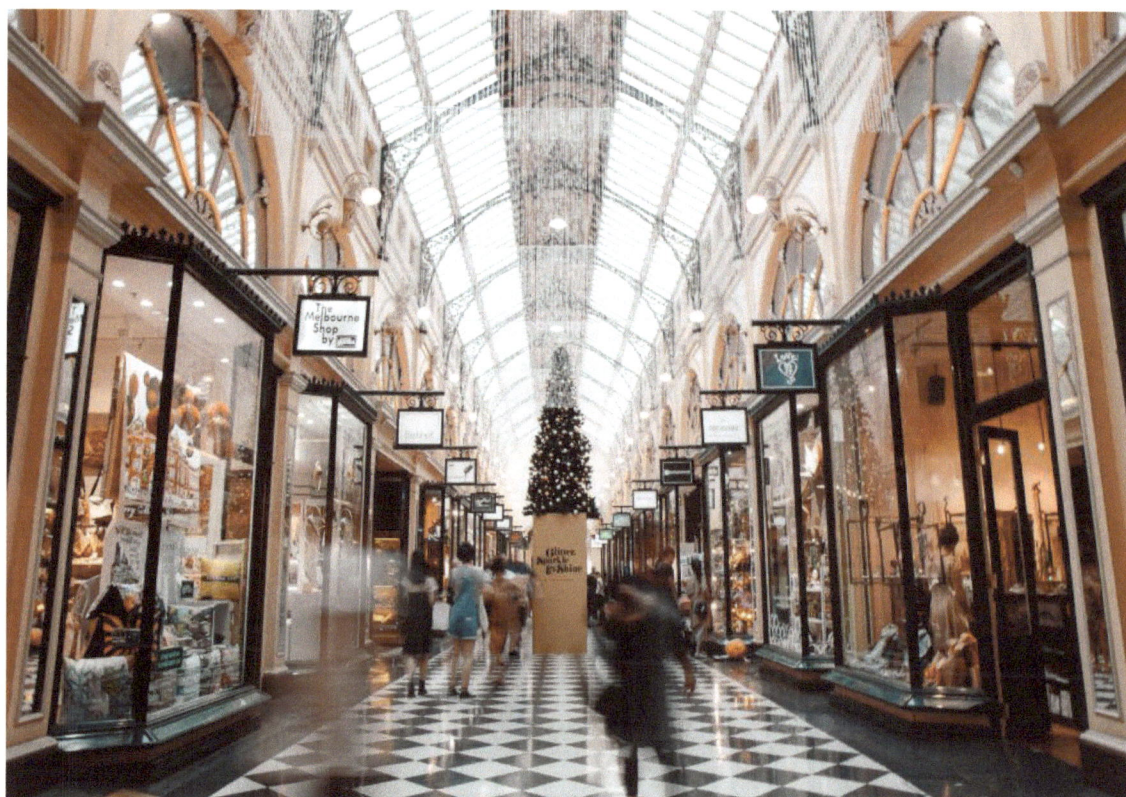

Outlet Centers: Usually located in rural, or occasionally, in tourist locations, outlet centers consist mostly of manufacturers' outlet stores selling their brands at a discount. These centers typically are not anchored.

Multifamily Rental Buildings

Many investors and real estate professionals start with the apartment buildings as an entry point to investment in commercial real estate. They feel comfortable with buildings comprised of 10 to 20 units because at some time in our lives, all of us have rented an apartment to live in, and we understand the utility bills, the maintenance, renter's insurance, paying the rent on time, and the consequences of being late. Beginner investors do not as easily understand the operation of an office building or a large shopping center.

When Apartment buildings have more than 60 units, things get a bit more complicated for the management, thus these are generally properties for investors with experience. Large apartment buildings are known as multifamily properties in commercial real estate. Multifamily buildings can be classified as follows:

Low Rise-Garden Type Apartments: Generally, these apartment buildings have one, two, or three floors and are set in an attractive garden area.

Mid-Rise Apartments:
These apartment buildings usually have between 4 and 8 floors, and have elevator service.

High-Rise Apartments:
Apartment buildings with more than 10 floors; in general, these have all modern comforts and amenities, as well as parking services and porterage.

Hospitality

A hotel is an establishment that offers accommodation and sometimes also includes meals, entertainment, and various personal services for the public.

"Real Capital Analytics" presents the following classification for the vastly different types of hospitality:

Limited service: These hotels, as the name indicates, do not have room service, don't have a restaurant, and do not offer concierge services. They are sometimes are referred to as "Express Inns."

Full Service: This type of Hospitality real estate comes with room service, restaurant service, and concierge service.

Boutique Hotel: A Boutique Hotel must meet the following conditions: be located in an urban area, provide full-service, generally have fewer than 200 rooms, and not be part of a national or international chain.

Casino Hotel: A hotel that has a casino on the premises is considered to be in this classification. Depending on the type of casino, in regard to its impact on income, the casino subtype is used instead of the plain Hotel classification.

Extended Stay Hotels: This type of hotel is also known as the apart-hotel. They provide a kitchen in the room, and the rooms are more spacious and comfortable.

Resort Hotel: A Resort hotel offers several amenities such as golf, water sports, and entertainment, providing for holiday stays. These hotels have large tracts of land for recreation, two or more swimming pools, and are generally located in cities where people go to vacation or on the beach.

Types of Hotel Suites: Suites offer more space and facilities to entertain, such as extra rooms, bars, etc. The previous classification is for hotels with more than 10 rooms, RCA type does not consider hotels or hostels with less than 10 rooms.

Special Purpose

Not all Special Purpose commercial properties fall into the above categories. This classification includes many uses, the more typical of which are mentioned below:
- **Hospitals**
- **Nursing Homes**
- **Marinas**
- **Movie Theaters**
- **Golf Courses**
- **Ranches**

Developable Land

Developable land is included in commercial real estate classifications, with the following uses:
- **Residential Buildings**
- **Residential Single Family Home Subdivisions**
- **Hotels**
- **Office Buildings**
- **Mixed Use**

- **Industrial Warehouses**
- **Shopping Centers**
- **Special Purpose**

Business

A businesses opportunity represents a "going concern." An interesting subdivision of commercial real estate practice, the going concern is conveyed based on the assumption that the entity will remain in business for the foreseeable future. Conversely, this means the entity will not be forced to halt operations and liquidate its assets in the near term at what may be very low fire-sale prices. A business can be purchased with or without the associated improved property. For ease of viewing we have subdivided the business into three types based on the size:

- **Small Businesses (< $200K)**
- **Medium Businesses ($ 200K - $ 750K)**
- **Large Businesses (> $ 750K)**

A business opportunity may have improved property associated with it. In other words, the owner of the business and the real estate improved property is the same. In this case, the business and the improved property must be analyzed separately. For the business, an EBITDA cash flow analysis for 5 to 10 years at the specific industry discount rate must be completed. The improved property must then be analyzed by considering the business fair market value rent.

If the Business Opportunity does not have real estate associated with it, and the business is leasing the property, an EBITDA cash flow analysis for 5 to 10 years at the particular industry discount rate must be completed. In this case, it is of critical importance to examine the terms of the lease agreement and incorporate the same including increases in income and how this may affect outcomes in the analysis.

EBITDA stands for: "Earnings Before Interest, Taxes, Depreciation, and Amortization"

It is important to mention that dealing with business opportunities is a specialty which requires extensive financial knowledge and negotiation experience. When representing the seller, the commercial practitioner must ask the seller for selected information such as the last three years' profit and loss statements, so a preliminary analysis of the chart of accounts can be done to verify the owner's benefits. Many business owners in special "Ma and Pa" businesses charge to the business expenses that are not related to the business itself, such as the car lease, life insurance, vacation trips, school tuition, etc. These items must be identified and added back to the bottom line. As a rule of thumb, the smaller the business, the more difficult it is to evaluate it.

When representing the buyer, we must analyze and understand all the expenses incurred and most importantly, the leasing contract. Buying a business because it is producing good money, while the lease term is only for two years would be a bad decision. The lease, or as defined as "the leasehold," of a business is an important asset of the firm.

Another important issue in dealing with business opportunities, is that some owners do not report cash income and it is not reflected in the books, but when they are ready to sell, they want this income taken into consideration.

In one of my deals, I was evaluating a hardware store business, and after detailing the chart of accounts and separating the owner's benefit, the valuation came to $395,000.

The asking price was $525,000 since the seller was counting income in cash that was not reflected in the profit and loss. I presented the financial analysis to my buyer, and I recommended that he place an offer for $395,000, which we did. Then the negotiation started. The seller was negotiating counting imaginary income, and I was negotiating on behalf of my client with facts. Since my client really liked the business, he decided to offer $425,000, which was finally accepted by the seller.

SECTION 2

The Ownership of Commercial Real Estate

Acquisition of Commercial Real Estate

There are two motivations to purchase commercial properties:

- Generation of income by rent and capital gains by the appreciation of the value of the property
- Operation of a business

Investment

Operate a Business

All investments must have an exit strategy, even though the initial strategy may change with time depending on different internal and external factors that have an effect on the investment. When you invest in a bank in an CD, you sign a contract for a period of time, usually one year, renewable. If you take your money before the expiration date and maturity of the CD, you will be penalized. In this case, your exit strategy is one year.

I have had very conservative investors who claimed that they do not want to provide an exit strategy since they are considering the investment as a way to build their family estate. They are never planning to sell. The problem is that without an exit strategy, you will not be able to evaluate the investment. I try to educate my investors, and I then tell them let's just pretend you will sell the property in 5 or 10 years; that way we can properly run the financial analysis and calculate the rate of return on the investment.

When you make an investment in commercial real estate, the retention period should be considered a priority. Real estate investors must include the amount of time of ownership of the asset. The time an investor anticipates keeping a property is called "The Holding Period."

The leasing of commercial properties is generally for longer periods than residential leasing. The length of commercial leases varies depending on the type of tenant, for example, three to five years for a small business to ten or more years for a major commercial company. Moving business and/or offices is generally expensive, and if the location brand association is important, long leases are the norm. Stability is good for owners and tenants alike.

If a commercial owner has prospective tenants who want short retention periods, the owner may want to include annual increases in their leases. This would help to increase net income and therefore the increase the value of the property.

Commercial mortgages for investment have maturities no more than 10 years. Thus, long term leases are a must for the investment. As already mentioned, relocation costs are considerable; therefore, it is economically reasonable to lease properties that meet the needs for a long-term.

In general, retention or holding periods for commercial real estate investments are for 5 to 10 years depending on the type of property and the financial planning of the investor.

Estate Planning

Considerations for succession planning often come into play when a property owner makes certain commercial investment decisions. For example, it is possible that an owner wants to transfer property to a family member, such as a child or a grandchild. You do not have to be an expert in estate planning, but it is very important to be aware of the regulations in your country, and look for advice with the appropriate professional.

The Objective of the Investment

As a commercial advisor, you need to know the investment goals of the client. It is of the utmost importance that you take the time to understand the investment objectives of the client. An investor in commercial real estate could have any of the following goals:

1. A building 100% rented that can provide a constant cash flow.
2. A building with potential, that with some updates and new tenants, could provide higher income for rent.
3. A building in poor condition, which can be renewed and be sold, thus generating a quick return: also known as a "Flip."
4. A building that does not generate much rent but that probably would appreciate substantially in value over time.
5. A building or land that can have the existing use/zoning changed.

Location, Location, Location…

As always, the location is a key factor. You've heard it again and again: real estate is location, location, location. In commercial real estate, the attraction of the location of the property depends largely on the type of building. For example, if it is an Office Building, easy access to public transport could be a must-have. If it is an Industrial Building, the value of the location is based on sources of employment and means of cargo transportation, such as rail, maritime, etc. If it is a Multifamily Building, then schools, recreation sites, and nearby shopping facilities would be of importance.

Local zoning is vital for the investor, especially if there is interest in extending a commercial building or changing the use.

A study serves to assess the value and demand for rental space. If an investor wishes to evaluate the property and the demand for rental of space for a building, you can assist your customer by preparing a market study. The data and the conclusions of a market study may be useful in the development of a business plan for your rental property.

The market study must include the following:

1. The total number of SF available in the market.
2. The total number of SF occupied in the market.
3. The asking rents per SF for the commercial spaces currently available.
4. The rent per SF, for the commercial spaces recently rented in the market.
5. Time on the market before being leased.
6. Concessions offered to the tenants of commercial spaces in the market.
7. Graphics with driving times.
8. Demographics of the area.

The basic elements of an investment in commercial real estate are cash inflows (rents), outflows (operating expenses and debt service), holding period, and risk. The ability to analyze these elements is fundamental in providing services to investors in commercial real estate.

Cash inflows and outflows are the money that is put into, or received from, the property including the original purchase cost and sale revenue over the entire life of the investment. An example of this sort of investment is a real estate fund.

Cash inflows include the following:
Rent
Additional rent to offset operating expenses
Fees: Parking, vending, services, etc.
Proceeds from sale
Tax benefits
Depreciation

Cash outflows include:
Initial investment (down payment plus associated acquisition costs)

All operating expenses and taxes
Debt service (mortgage payment)
Capital expenses and tenant leasing costs
Sales costs

The timing of cash inflows and outflows is necessary to building a "T Chart" showing cash flows over time. Risk is dependent on market conditions, current tenants, and the likelihood that they will renew their leases year-after-year. It is important to be able to predict the probability of realizing those cash inflows and accounting for the outflows, so that the probability of maintaining those amounts on time, including vacancy factors can provide a realistic projection of what is to come.

Commercial Real Estate offers a pride of ownership factor that is nearly impossible to value, but is, nevertheless, one of the highest among all asset classes. There is great joy and pleasure in knowing you own an income-producing property…a piece of the commerce and business activity that drives the economic engine of the world. The ownership of commercial real estate presents several advantages:

Appreciation

Historically, Commercial Real Estate Investments have provided excellent appreciation in value that meets and exceeds other investment types. The value of real property is generally driven up by internal and external factors. Among the internal factors are: optimum management, improvements not to defer any required maintenance, reduced administrative costs and the maintainence of excellent landlord/tenant relationships. External factors include supply and demand as well as the desirablity of locations.

Regular Income Stream

One of the biggest benefits to Commercial Real Estate Investments is that assets are generally secured by leases, which provide a regular income stream, significantly higher than typical stock dividend yields.

Accumulate Equity by Amortization of the Debt.

Leverage allows you to place debt on the improved property, which is several times the original equity. This lets you buy more assets with less money and significantly magnifies your equity as the loans are paid down.

Superior Hedge Against Inflation

According to a recent report by expert, Martha S. Peyton, Ph.D., head of the Global Real Estate Strategy for TIAA-CREF, commercial real estate investments had the highest correlation to inflation when compared to other asset classes such as the S&P 500, ten year Treasury notes, and corporate bonds. As the United States, Asia, and Europe continue to carry out policies allowing them to print more money as a spur to economic growth, it is important to recognize the benefits of owning commercial real estate as a hedge against inflation.

Liquidity vs Hard Asset

While brick & mortar is not a liquid asset, Commercial Real Estate is one of the few investment classes that is a hard asset that also has meaningful intrinsic value. The property's land has value, as does the improved property itself.

Tax Benefits

The US Tax code benefits real estate owners in several ways. For instance, mortgage interest and depreciation deductions can shield a large portion of your income stream. Also useful for protecting your income is Internal Revenue Code 1031, known as 1031 exchange, under which the investor may defer recognition of capital gains and related federal income tax liability on the exchange of like-kind properties.

Leveraging

Real estate assets are typically expensive in comparison to other widely available investment instruments such as stocks or bonds. But only rarely will real estate investors pay the entire amount of the purchase price of a property in cash. Usually, a large portion of the purchase price will be financed using some sort of financial instrument or debt, such as a mortgage loan collateralized by the property itself. The amount of the purchase price financed by debt is referred to as leverage. The amount financed by the investor's own capital, through cash or other asset transfers, is referred to as equity.

The ratio of leverage to total appraised value (often referred to as "LTV," or loan to value for a conventional mortgage) is one mathematical measure of the risk an investor is taking by using leverage to finance the purchase of a property. Investors usually seek to decrease their equity requirements and increase their leverage, so that their return on investment (ROI) is maximized. Lenders and other financial institutions usually have minimum equity requirements for real estate investments they are being asked to finance, typically on the order of 20% of appraised value. Investors seeking low equity requirements may explore alternate financing arrangements as part of the purchase of a property (for instance, seller financing, seller subordination, private equity sources, etc.)

If the property requires substantial repair, traditional lenders like banks will often not lend on a property and the investor may be required to borrow from a private lender using a short-term bridge loan like a Hard money loan from a Hard money lender. Hard money loans are usually short term loans

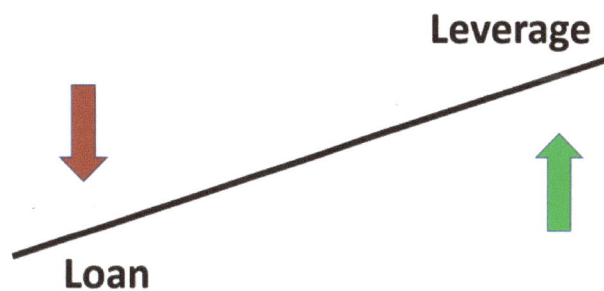

for which the lender charges a much higher interest rate because of the higher risk nature of the loan. Hard money loans are typically at a much lower Loan-to-value ratio than conventional mortgages.

Some real estate investment organizations, such as real estate investment trusts (REITs) and some pension funds and Hedge funds, have large enough capital reserves and investment strategies to allow 100% equity in the properties that they purchase. This minimizes the risk which comes from leverage, but also limits potential ROI.

By leveraging the purchase of an investment property, the required periodic payments to service the debt create an ongoing (and sometimes large) negative cash flow beginning from the time of purchase. This is sometimes referred to as the carry cost or "carry" of the investment. To be successful, real estate investors must manage their cash flows to create enough positive income from the property to at least offset the carry costs.

Title, Surveying, Environmental Considerations

Investing in commercial real estate requires performing a detailed investigation of the survey of the property. Does it have any encroachments? Does it have any easements? Does it have any liens? Does it have any open permits? Does it have any violations? Does it have the correct zoning and use? All of these tasks are usually performed by the attorney and/or the closing company.

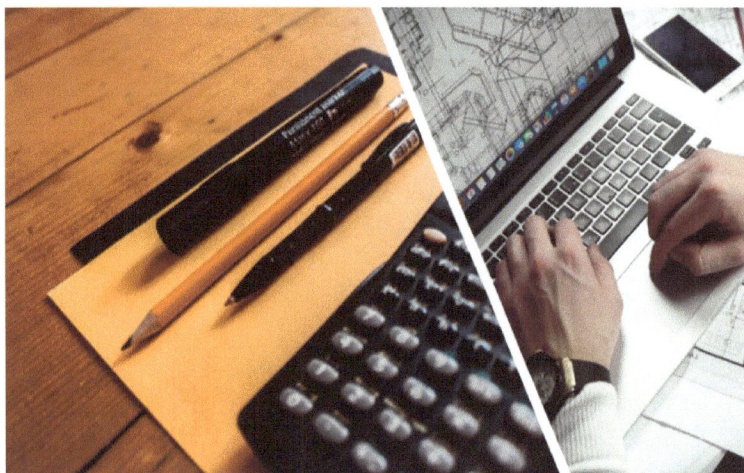

You must also take a closer look at the topographical map of the property and review any bondage included or excluded. An easement gives the right to use the land of another for a particular purpose. For example, an easement could give an owner the right to use an entry to an adjacent property. Easements may limit the possibilities for expansion of a property. This "bondage" has to be taken into consideration.

Investors need to know whether the property has appropriate connections for sewage. There are state and local regulations applicable to waste systems, such as septic tanks. A property with a waste system must be inspected before the title property can be transferred. This type of inspection is mandatory in some jurisdictions.

If the customer is going to buy a property, the offer to purchase should include a contingency clause in case of unforeseen circumstances in which it is found that the property is not compatible with the existing systems of final disposal.

If the client is selling a property that has a system of final waste, the client should hire an inspector to review the system of elimination before placing the property on the market. This could alleviate concerns that potential buyers might have on the disposal system.

Hazardous waste laws vary depending on the state and local jurisdictions. Depending on local regulations, the remediation of contamination can be extremely costly. In the United States, there are severe penalties for owners who do not resolve these situations. In some states, when the hazardous waste is not cleaned up, a lien can be placed on the property, and each of the parties involved is responsible, including the previous owners. Damages can be imposed without regard to fault, and the state can repossess the property.

An offer to purchase should include a contingency linked to an assessment of hazardous wastes, which gives the buyer the right to choose a licensed site professional (LSP) to carry out the evaluation. If the evaluation reveals that hazardous waste is contaminating the property, the buyer can cancel the transaction.

The environmental study consists of three phases if these become necessary. For example, if Phase I finds no evidence of contamination, it is not necessary go to Phase II.

Phase I focuses on the following:

Exploring the current and historical uses of the property.

Searching for evidence that hazardous materials have been handled on the property.

Discovering whether the property is under federal or state jurisdiction relative to the environment.

Finding out if hazardous materials have spilled on nearby properties.

In the second phase, water samples and soil are collected and analyzed. Phase II is much more extensive and costly, and may not be necessary if the lender and the buyer are satisfied with the findings of Phase I.

Assessments involving hazardous waste are beyond the experience of most real estate practitioners. Therefore, as problems arise during the evaluation, the agent should suggest that customers consult with lawyers, environmental professionals, accountants, and insurance agents to ensure that they get expert advice.

When representing a buyer or a seller, the commercial practitioner must advise the buyer to perform an Environmental Phase I and Phase II evaluation if necessary.

When the purchase is going to be financed, the financial institution will make require an assessment of the environment as mandatory in getting the loan. If the purchase is going to be a cash transaction, the buyer may not order an environmental assessment. I represented a buyer a few years back who was buying a warehouse for cash and after much advise on my part, he decided not to have the environmental assessment. In order to avoid a liability issue, I had my buyer sign a document I had prepared indicating that I had advised him to order the study, and he refused to do it.

Conclusion:

Unlike stocks, commercial real estate investments often provide stable cash flows in the form of rental income. Commercial real estate is a hard asset that is also a scarce resource. It always has some intrinsic value, and usually appreciates in value over time. Finally, the value of commercial real estate is derived by the larger growth of the economy.

Important Concepts

In this section we will define the relevant financial concepts involved in commercial real estate investment as well as the relation between them and how to calculate each of them.

Potential Gross Income ("PGI")

Potential gross income (also known as PGI or gross potential rent) is the total revenue a property could generate if 100% leased at market rent. PGI reflects the most annual rent a property would collect.

Effective Gross Income ("EGI")

Effective Gross Income (or EGI) represents the PGI plus any additional rent subject to vacancy, minus the vacancy and the credit losses.

Gross Operating Income ("GOI")

Gross Operating Income (or GOI) represents the Effective Gross Operating Income (EGI) plus any additional rent not subject to vacancy, such as a rent generated by a billboard or a cell tower.

Operating Expenses ("OE")

Operating Expenses (or OE) are all the direct expenses related to the operation of the building.

Debt Service ("DS")

Debt Service is the annual loan payment.

Net Operating Income ("NOI")

Net Operating Income (or NOI) is the net income generated by an investment property excluding the debt service. In other words, NOI is the cash flow generated by rents on a property owned free and clear.

Capitalization Rate ("CAP Rate")

The capitalization rate is defined as the ratio of the Net Operating Income and the Value of the property.

Net Cash Flow ("NCF")

The Net Cash Flow ("NCF") is the net income that results from subtracting the debt service from the NOI.

Return on Investment ("ROI")

Investors need to know the potential return that an investment in commercial real estate would produce. When contemplating the purchase of a commercial property, the investor will pay particular attention to the rate of return on investment (ROI) as compared with the cost of money. The greater the return on the investment, the higher the value of the property. The ROI is calculated as the ratio between the net cash flow divided by the initial investment, II.

Initial Investment (II)

It is the initial investment paid for a property, including all the closing expenses in the period "0".

It is important to quantify the above concepts in a table called "Annual Property Operating Data" or APOD where the different variables are calculated.

ANNUAL PROPERTY OPERATING DATA

Owner/Investor		Purchase Price	
Location:		Acquisition Costs	
Type of Property		Mortgage Points	
Size of Property (SF or Units)		Down Payment	
		Initial Investment	

Assessed Value	$	%
Land		
Improved Property		
Total		

	INCOME		COMMENTS
1	POTENTIAL GROSS (RENTAL) INCOME		
2	+ Other Income (affected by vacancy)		
3	"- Vacancy & Credit Losses		
4	EFFECTIVE GROSS (RENTAL) INCOME		
5	+ Other Income (not affected by vacancy)		
6	GROSS OPERATING INCOME		
	OPERATING EXPENSES		
7	Real Estate Taxes		
8	Personal Property Taxes		
9	Property Insurance		
10	Offsite Management		
11	Payroll		
12	Expenses/Benefits		
13	Taxes/Worker's Compensation		
14	Repairs and Maintenance		
	Utilities		
15	Electric		
16	Water		
17	Gas		
18	Cable		
19	Accounting and Legal		
20	Licenses/Permits		
21	Advertising		
22	Supplies		
	Contract Services		
24	Landscaping		
25	Porter Service		
26	Waste Management		
27			
28			
29	TOTAL OPERATING EXPENSES		
30	NET OPERATING INCOME		
31	- Debt Service		
32	- Reserves		
33	- Leasing Commissions		
34	- Capital Additions		
35	CASH FLOW BEFORE TAXES		

$$\text{GOI} - \text{OE} = \text{NOI}$$

$$\text{NOI} - \text{DS} = \text{NCF}$$

$$\text{NCF} \div \text{II} = \text{ROI}$$

Example 3.1:

Peter wants to make an investment in commercial real estate and is looking to buy a commercial retail premise which generates a monthly income of $5,000.00, the annual operating expenditure of the property is $8,000. The price of the property is $500,000 and the investor wants to place 30% down. Peter goes to a local bank and secures a loan for $350,000 with monthly payments of $2,300. If Peter wants to get an ROI of a 15 %, should he proceed with the transaction?

Please try it to resolve it using the formulas presented, answer is at the end of the book.

Example 3.3:

Mary would like to purchase a 10-unit multifamily building, composed of six1-bedroom units and four 2-bedroom units. Rents for the -1-bedroom units are $1,000 each and for the 2-bedroom units are

$1,500. Currently, there is a vacancy of one 2-bedroom unit. Operating expenses are estimated at 30% of the Potential Gross Income. If Mary want a return on investment of 9%, How much Mary can offer for the building?

Please try it to resolve it using the formulas presented, answer is at the end of the book.

Example 3.4:

Henry wants to invest in commercial real estate. He has $500,000 available to invest, and he has been presented with two options: to buy one property with $500,000 cash and no leverage or to buy two properties of $1,000,000 each with $750,000 leverage each. What would you recommend that Henry do?

Scenario 1- Buy One Property
Price
Initial Investment $500,000
NOI $ 35,000

Scenario 1- Buy Two Properties
Property 1 $1,000,000
Initial Investment $ 250,000
Loan $ 750,000
NOI $ 70,000
Debt Service $ 56,396

Property 2 $1,000,000
Initial Investment $ 250,000
Loan $ 750,000
NOI $ 75,000
Debt Service $ 56,396

Please try it to resolve it using the formulas presented, answer is at the end of the book.

Estimating Value of Commercial Property

Valuation of commercial property

Valuation methods of real estate and businesses are similar. Valuation is a key consideration for investors in commercial real estate. If your investor is considering purchasing improved property or a business, an analysis must be carried out to estimate the value of the investment. There are three methods to estimate value of commercial properties:

1. The Method of Comparable Sales

2. The Method of Cost Analysis (Reposition or Replacement)

3. The Method of Income.

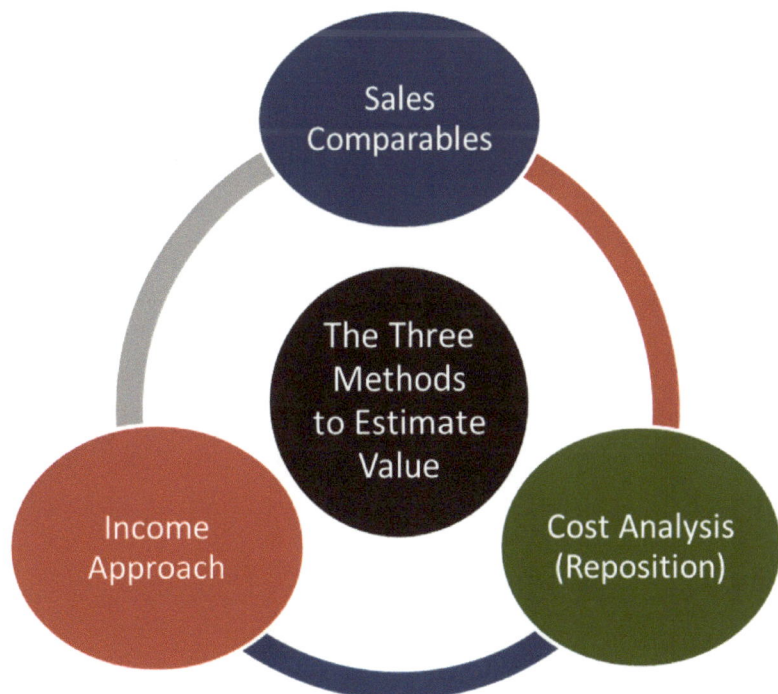

1. Sales Comparable Approach

This equates the prices of properties that buyers have historically paid for similar properties. It is like the "comparable purchase" when a consumer compares the price of a particular article in several shops to determine what price should be paid for the same item. In the world of real estate, however, there are no two identical properties. The following is the procedure for applying this method:

a. Find properties of the ***same category and class*** that have sold recently in the free market.

b. Adjust the comparable for each variant.

c. Make net adjustments.

d. Get an average of the comparable representative properties, and discard those that go outside of a reasonable range for comparison, both high and low.

This method is effective when a representative number of properties sold recently is available, indicative of an active market.

2. Cost Reposition Approach

This method is also known as the replacement method, it is based on establishing the costs of the same property and subtracting the depreciation of the same. Depreciation can come from three sources: physical deterioration, physical obsolescence, and external obsolescence. These terms are defined as:

Physical Deterioration:	Wear/deterioration due to normal use of the property.
Physical Obsolescence:	The inability of the building to provide the same utility and services that could be offered by a newly purpose-built property.
External Obsolescence:	Loss in value due to external factors. For example, the zone has been depressed economically, etc.

The following is the procedure for applying this method:

a. Estimate the cost to build the same property.
b. Estimate the cost of different forms of depreciation
c. Calculate the total depreciation
d. Estimate the value of the land
e. Add the value of the land to the depreciated value.

This method is of great interest when attempting to set a ceiling on the value of the property, since no buyer will be willing to pay an amount greater than the cost of replacement of a brand-new building. One limitation, however, is that it does not take into account factors of supply and demand. It is not recommended if the degree of depreciation is very high. Evaluators typically use this method when:

- There is a lack of data on comparables available in the market.
- The building is of particular use, with few comparable properties.
- The property is a new construction

3. Income Approach

The most popular type is the income approach, which is based on the evaluation of income. This method is based on the premise that there is a correlation between an income producing property and its value. There are two methods based on the income of the property:

- **Method of Direct Capitalization**
- **Discounted Cash-flow**

The Method of Direct Capitalization

Capitalization Rate

In fact, there are two methods of valuation based on income: the method of capitalization (Capitalization Rate) and gross income multiplier. The capitalization rate is the most popular method of the two. With the capitalization rate, the market value of the property is calculated by dividing the net operating income (NOI) by the capitalization rate.

NOI, is obtained by subtracting the operating costs of the total gross revenue.

The capitalization rate (CAP Rate) is the overall performance of the investment. The CAP Rate can be calculated by dividing NOI by the sale price of the property.

$$ NOI \div CAP = Value $$

Gross Income Multiplier

The "Gross Income Multiplier" ("GIM"), also called Gross Revenue Multiplier" ("GRM") is used to evaluate apartment buildings and hotels.

The disadvantage of this method is that it does not take into consideration operating expenses of the property and unemployment.

$$ Sale\ Price \div GOI = GIM $$

Discounted Cash-Flow Method

This model is based on discounting the future value of income when compared to the present value. Unlike the capitalization method, which provides a snapshot at a given time, the discounted cash flow method allows us to know the flow of revenues and expenditures during a period. The period is generally set for five to ten years.

The value of the property is defined:

• By holding all the NOI until the end of the period
• Projecting the sale value of the property to the end of the period

N	$	
0	(VP)	
1	NOI	
2	NOI	
	NOI	
	NOI	
N	NOI	+ Sale Net Proceeds

Procedure

a. Project the NOI for each year of the period
b. Estimate the value of sale at the end of the period
c. Determine the desired rate of discount for the investor
d. Solve for NPV

The discounted cash-flow method considers the desired rate of the investor. It is the more accurate method for evaluating an investment property. Stable properties can be analyzed by the capitalization method, while properties which are expected to produce variable cash flows or to be acquired by sophisticated investors must be analyzed by the discounted cash flow method.

IMPORTANT:

THE DISCOUNT RATE IS NOT THE SAME AS THE CAPITALIZATION RATE. DISCOUNT RATES ARE THE RATES DESIRED BY THE INVESTOR, AND ARE USED TO CONVERT A STREAM OF FUTURE INCOME OVER THE NET INCOME FROM SALES PROJECTED TO PRESENT VALUE.

THE CAPITALIZATION RATE IS COMPUTED BY DIVIDING THE NOI BY THE SELLING PRICE OF A COMPARABLE RECENTLY SOLD.

$$NPV = -II + \frac{C1}{1+r} + \frac{C2}{(1+r)^2} + \frac{C3}{(1+r)^T}$$

Co = Initial Investment
C = Cash Flow
r = Discount Rate
T = Time

Using the method of Net Present Value, future cash flows are discounted to current value using the appropriate discount rate.

The discount rate for an investor represents the opportunity cost for each individual investor or the weighted average cost used by corporate investors.

From the point of view of an individual investor, the discount rate represents the performance that might be obtained in an alternative investment. This rate is referred to as the desired rate of the investor or the rate performance object.

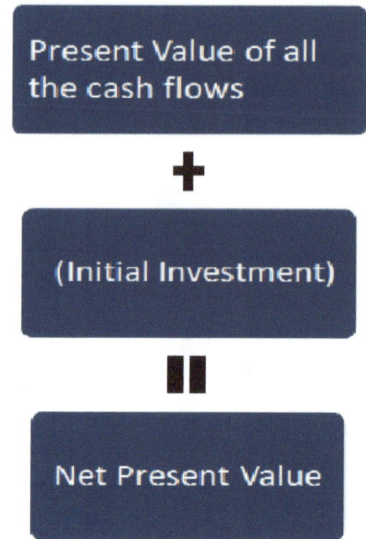

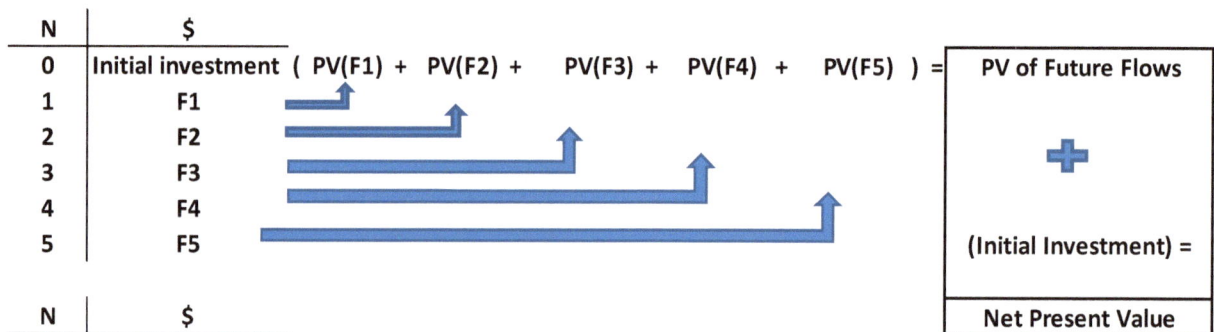

Present Value of all the cash flows

+

(Initial Investment)

=

Net Present Value

N	$							
0	Initial investment (PV(F1) + PV(F2) + PV(F3) + PV(F4) + PV(F5)) =							PV of Future Flows
1	F1							
2	F2							**+**
3	F3							
4	F4							
5	F5							(Initial Investment) =
N	$							Net Present Value

There are two methods to calculate the Net Present Value. The first deals with each cash flow individually associated with the present value, that is each flow of each period is discounted to its present value and subsequently added to the initial investment to get the Net Present Value. The second method uses the routine of the cash flows of the financial calculator or an Excel spreadsheet.

To illustrate both methods to calculate the Net Present Value, we will solve the following example.

Example 4.1 Determine the Net Present Value

For a better understanding of the two methods calculate the following: a buyer has an initial investment of $10,000 in an investment that produces the following cash flows:

N	$
0	-9,000
1	1,000
2	2,000
3	4,000
4	5,000

The desired investor rate is 7 %, what would be the Net Present Value of this investment?

Method 1:

Step 1. We set up the T-bar

Step 2. We calculate the present values of each individual cash flow,
by entering the future value, the term of periods and the desired interest rate by an investor.

For	$1,000	$ 934.58
For	$2,000	$1,746.88
For	$4,000	$3,265.19
For	$5,000	$3,815.24

Step 3. Add all the present values for the cash flows, Total is $9,761.89

Step 4. We add the sum of the present values to the initial investment.
And the NPV results in $9,761.89 - $9,000= $761.89

Method 2:

Step 1. We set up the T-bar

N	$
0	-9,000
1	1,000
2	2,000
3	4,000
4	5,000

Step 2. We calculate with our financial calculator the NPV of the future cash flows discounted at 7%.
NPV = $761.12

+   Edit   Share   Graph   Done

Cash Flows - Payments p...

Amount:	-9000		Initial Cash Flow

Amount:	1000	# Times:	1
Amount:	2000	# Times:	1
Amount:	4000	# Times:	1
Amount:	5000	# Times:	1

¤761.12   ¤997.68

NPV   NFV   IRR/YR

Positive Net Present Value

A positive present value indicates that the yield is greater than the desired rate. In the example above the positive value of the Net Present Value of $761.12, indicates that the investor could have paid up to $9,761.12 for the investment, by obtaining the same desired rate.

Negative Net Present Value

If, in the previous example, we change the desired rate of the investor from 7% to 12 %, the Net Present Value would be - $488.04, and in this case, the investor could have paid $8,511.96 ($9,000 - $ 488.04) to obtain the desired investment.

Net Present Value

NPV would be zero at the maximum rate that it could obtain the investor without paying on the initial investment. If, in the previous example, we run the cash flows, and we put the PV to zero, we obtain the optimal performance sought: 9.93%.

If the Net Present Value is:	The Investor Will Get
Positive	More than the desired rate of return
Negative	Less than the desired rate of return
Zero	The desired rate of return

Example 4.2

Mary wants to buy a commercial property that will produce reasonable income for her retirement. She contacts a residential real estate consultant, and he refers her to a commercial real estate consultant. Mary holds a meeting with the commercial broker and gives him the following information:

1. Plans to retire in about 6 months.
2. Requires a monthly net income of $10,000. Has $1,000,000 in savings to invest.
3. Wants to see properties that meet these requirements.

If the average capitalization rates in the area where Mary wants to buy are at 14% what would you advise your customer?

Please try it to resolve this using the formulas presented; answer is at the end of the book.

Example 4.3

John owns two commercial properties: a warehouse and a retail space. Both have appreciated substantially in recent years. The warehouse produces a net income of $10,000 per month and the retail space generates a net income of $8,000 per month. John would like to find out if it is possible to sell the two properties and acquire a shopping center in the area that is newly built and fully rented with net income of $ 40/SF with increases of 5% per annum. The shopping center has a total of 6000 SF. The objective of John is that within two years after he retires, he will receive a monthly income of $20,000.00.

Based on the following premises, what would you advise to John?

TCAP
Building   15%
Retail/Shopping Center   12%

What would you advise John?

Please try it to resolve it using the formulas presented, answer is at the end of the book.

Example 4.4

You have been hired by a corporation to rent 20,000 SF of Class A office space in the Brickell area in Miami, FL. The corporation notifies you that they have budgeted a net monthly rent not to exceed $30.00 per SF per year. However, until now they have been talking to some people and the rents seem to be in the range of $40.00 to $50.00 per SF per year. In order to be able to pay more than the budgeted price, they must have authorization from corporate headquarters in Dallas, Texas. To get this, they need to present an analysis showing the market conditions, which you have been asked to prepare:

Under the following assumptions, would you be able to prepare the report requested?

It has been determined that in the past six months, 7 Class A office buildings have been sold as follows:

Building	Sale Price	Area SF	Date
A	$ 29,000,000.00	100,000	15-Jan-15
B	$ 59,000,000.00	140,000	5-Mar-15
C	$ 51,000,000.00	110,000	19-Apr-15
D	$ 34,000,000.00	75,000	9-Feb-15
E	$ 38,000,000.00	85,000	19-Jan-15
F	$ 27,000,000.00	105,000	1-May-15
G	$ 31,500,000.00	70,000	21-Jan-15

Also, the following NNN rents in the area of Brickell for class A buildings were determined.

Building	Monthly NNN Rents	Area SF	Date
1	$ 70,000.00	17,500	15-Jan-13
2	$ 42,000.00	15,000	5-Mar-14
3	$ 5,000.00	2,000	19-Apr-14
4	$ 14,250.00	5,000	9-Feb-13
5	$ 20,625.00	9,000	19-Jan-14
6	$ 35,000.00	12,000	1-May-13
7	$ 50,000.00	20,000	21-Jan-15

What is the CAP rate?

Please try it to resolve this using the formulas presented; answer is at the end of the book.

Financing Commercial Property

Commercial real estate properties are financed with commercial real estate loans: mortgage loans secured by liens on the commercial property. Loans are issued by Financial Institutions, Insurance Companies, Pension Funds, Private Investors, and other sources of capital. .

It is important to differentiate between commercial loans for an owner/user versus commercial loans for an investor. Owner/user loans are less risky to lending institutions than are loans for investment properties. In fact, the U.S. Small Business Administration oversees the 504 Loan program, wherein the buyer is required to put down only 10% of the purchase price. On the other hand, the buyer will have to put down between 25% to 50% for investment properties, depending on the transaction.

Commercial loans differ from residential loan in interest rates and in the maturity of the term of the loan. Commercial loans (with the exception of SBA loans) though they may be amortized in 20 to 25 years, have maturity terms between 7 and 10 years. A lender, for example, might make a commercial loan for a term of seven years with an amortization period of 20 years. In this situation, the investor would make payments for seven years of an amount based on the loan being paid off over 30 years, followed by one final "balloon" payment of the entire remaining balance on the loan. The length of the loan term and the amortization period will affect the rate the lender charges. Depending on the investor's credit strength, these terms may be negotiable. In general, the longer the loan repayment schedule, the higher the interest rate.

Loan-to-Value Ratios, LTV

The LTV is calculated by dividing the amount of the loan by the lesser of the property's appraised value or purchase price. For example, the LTV for a $700,000 loan on a $1,000,000 property would be 70% ($70,000 ÷ $1,000,000 = 0.7, or 70%).

Debt Service

Deb Service is the amount of principal plus interest paid in one year. In other words, debt service is the monthly payment times twelve months.

$$DS = PMT \times 12$$

Debt-Service Coverage Ratio

Commercial lenders also look at the debt-service coverage ratio (DSCR), which compares a property's annual net operating income (NOI) to its annual mortgage debt service. It represents a risk mitigation percentage. Depending on the markets and the financial institutions, this ratio can vary from 1.25 to 1.4. It is calculated by dividing the NOI by the annual debt service.

$$DSCR = NOI \div DS$$

Interest Rates and Fees

Interest rates on commercial loans are generally higher than on residential loans. Also, commercial real estate loans usually involve fees that add to the overall cost of the loan, including appraisal, legal, loan application, loan origination, and/or survey fees. Some costs must be paid up front before the loan is approved (or rejected), while others apply annually. For example, a loan may have a one-time loan origination fee of 1.5%, due at the time of closing, and an annual fee of 0.30% until the loan is fully paid.

Prepayment

A commercial real estate loan may have restrictions on prepayment. This is to guarantee that the lender will get its desired yield on the loan.

There are different types of commercial loans:

Commercial Conventional Loans:

Conventional commercial loans are mortgages that are provided by a bank, credit union, savings institution, or other traditional financial institution. They are secured by a first lien position on the properties being financed. These loans are typically best suited for inexperienced borrowers, and are usually used for properties with small loan balances, for specialty properties, and for other structures that may require a personal guaranty.

Usually between $500,000 and $5,000,000, these loans are based on both the financial ability of the property to generate enough income stream to cover the debt service and the track record or credit history of the individual who will be guaranteeing the loan. These loans are referred to as "Recourse Loans."

Commercial Mortgage Backed Securities Loan, "CMBS":

CMBS loans, as the name indicates, are loans backed by security instruments that are funded by a pool of investors. Also called Conduit Loans, these are packaged into a pool with other similar type commercial loans and sold to institutional investors. The loans in the pool serve as collateral for the mortgage backed security. A CMBS Loan has a fixed interest rate (which may or may not include an interest-only period) and is typically amortized over 25-30 years with a balloon payment due at the end of the term, which is usually ten (10) years. Because the loans are not held on the Conduit Lender's balance sheet, CMBS Loans are a great way for these lenders to provide an additional loan product to borrowers while at maintaining their liquidity position. Because of more flexible underwriting guidelines, CMBS Loans also allow commercial real estate investors that cannot meet stringent conventional liquidity and net worth guidelines to be able to invest in commercial real estate. CMBS loans are "Non-Recourse Loans," meaning the borrower is not required to personally guarantee the loan. These types of loans cannot be prepaid in the first two years and after the second year have a pre-payment penalty called defeasance.

Defeasance.

Defeasance allows the borrower to purchase substitute collateral for the conduit loan. The pool of investors or bondholders are expecting a certain rate of return from their investment in a CMBS commercial loan, therefore the loan cannot be paid back within the first two (2) years after the loan origination. After that two-year "lock-out period," the loan can be repaid by substituting the CMBS loan and its stipulated interest rate with a portfolio of high-quality bonds (usually U.S. Treasury bonds) to make up the desired yield of the investors. Defeasance is a complex process generally structured by financial advisors and experienced attorneys.

Life Insurance Loans:

Another option is to borrow money from insurance companies. In most cases, they may offer favorable terms if the borrower can demonstrate a decent NOI. As with any investor, insurance loans require a more conservative loan to value (LTV) with maximums for most lenders between 60-75%, and debt service coverage ratios (DSCRs) of at least 1.25-1.35. Prior commercial real estate ownership or experience with a professional management company is highly desirable. The term from these loans may vary from 7 – 30 years with amortizations ranging between 15 to 30 years. As in the previous types, depending on the way the loan is structured, it may have a "balloon" at maturity. Life insurance loans may be non-recourse, limited recourse, or full recourse loans. However, in the event the Borrower commits loan fraud, property transfer or subordinate financing without consent of the Lender, the borrower may become personal liable for the loan.

Loan Assumption:

The vast majority of life insurance loans and CMBS loans are assumable, typically for a fee. This can occur when the Borrower wants to sell the commercial real estate that secures the loan, and the buyer of the property wants to take over the loan. The benefit of this structure is that the buyer will pay lower closing costs and the assumable loan may also have more favorable terms than are available at market. Loan assumption is an especially attractive option in high interest rate or tight credit environments.

Loan Calculations

It is crucial to understand the financial calculations of commercial loans. From simple calculations to calculating the payment amount or the balloon at the mature date/sale date, as well as performin sensibility analyses for different interest rates and LTV ratios. We will present some examples to illustrate these loan calculations:

5.1 An investor wants to purchase a strip center for $3,000,000. He visited his local bank to get a conventional commercial loan, and the lending officer gave him the estimated basic terms as follows:

LTV	70%
Interest Rate	5.25%
Term	7 years
Amortization	25 years

The mortgage will be 70% of the purchase price.

Loan Amount	$2,100,000

Using the financial calculator, the monthly payment amortized at 25 years will be:

PMT (Monthly Payment)	-$12,584.20 (It is negative because it is a disbursement for the borrower).
Debt Service	-$151,010.40
Balloon at Maturity (7 years)	-$1,756,088.83

5.2 The investor above, gets detailed financial information regarding the strip center, and goes again to his local bank and presents the information to the loan officer. The loan officer looks at the property income and determines that the NOI is $180,000, at a 15% vacancy rate. The average retail vacancy in the area is 10%. The loan officer tells the investor that the bank will consider the loan but a DSCR of 1.3 must be met.

Based on the DSCR of 1.3, the new Debt Service must be calculated as:

New Debt Service $180,000/1.3 = $138,461.54 and the PMT,

PMT $11,538.46

Resulting in a New Loan Amount of $1,925,491

Re-applying the same LTV of 70%, the value the property will support would be,

New Value $1,925,491/70% = $2,750,701

Based on this calculation the investor has two options:

1. To try to negotiate the price, asking for a discount of $250,000; or
2. To increase the down payment from $900,000 to $1,075,000, obtaining an adjusted LTV of 64.18%.

Looking at these two examples, it is important to note that the NOI of the property and the DSCR determine the value of the loan. If the calculation of the new loan had been higher, the one to take into consideration is the given for the 70% LTV.

In reference to the vacancy factor, not adjustment was made since the vacancy in the area is lower than the current vacancy of the property.

Example 5.3

An Investor, buys an apartment building for $1,500,000, and leverages the cost with 75% of the investment. The mortgage loan has the following conditions:

Term   25 years
Interest Rate   9%
Payments   12 per year

The first year, the investor receives a gross income of $175.000. This was not the anticipated vacancy for the first year. From the second year on, the vacancy is estimated at 5%, increasing the income by 3% per annum. If the expenditures for the first year are $10,000, and there will be an estimated 3% annual increase, prepare cash flow for the period. If it is estimated that the capitalization rate will be 10% at the end of the period, determine the sale value, considering the fact that you pay a commission of 5%.

(Prepare the model for 5 years)

Calculate the net present value at a discount rate (desired investor rate) of 11%. Calculate also the rate of return of the investment.

Mortgage	
Amount	$1,500 * .75 = $1,125,000
Term	25 years
Interest	9%
Payments	12
Monthly Payment	- $9,440.96
Annual Payment	- $113.292
Amortization	60 Months
Balloon at year 5	$1,049,315

The initial investment is $375,000 which is negative because represents an outflow or a disbursement.

Year 1

The NOI would be the income from rent, $175,000, minus $10,000 of the operating expenses

Year 2

The income from rent is increased in 3%, and is $180,250. But it is also affected by vacancy, resulting in $171,238. Operating expenses are increased in year 2 by 3% to $10,300. The NOI for year 2 would be 160,938.

Year 3

The income from rent is increased by 3%, and is $176,375. Operating expenses are increased in year 2 by 3% to $10,609. The NOI for year 3 would be $165,766.

Year 4

The income from rent is increased in 3%, and is $181,666. Operating expenses are increased in year 3 by 3% to $10,927. The NOI for year 4 would be 170,739.

Year 5

Year 5 has 2 streams of income, the one generated by rent and the one generated by the sales proceeds. The income from rent is increased by 3%, and is $187,116. Operating expenses are increased in year 3 by 3% to $11,255. The NOI for year 5 would be 175,861.

If we deduct now the debt service from each NOI, we will obtain the cash flows in the table for the 5-year period.

In addition, we have to take into consideration the net proceeds from the sale in year 5:

N	$	Net Flow less Debt Service	Net Flow end of the period
0	$ (375,000)	$ (375,000)	$ (375,000)
1	$ 165,000	$ 51,708	$ 51,708
2	$ 160,938	$ 47,646	$ 47,646
3	$ 165,766	$ 52,474	$ 52,474
4	$ 170,739	$ 57,447	$ 57,447
5	$ 175,861	$ 62,569	$ 683,933
Net Present Value			$192,346

Net Proceeds from Sale
Gross Sale Price $175,861 / 10% = $1,758,610
Sales Commissions (5 %) $87,931
Balance of the Mortgage $1,049,315
Net Income of the Sale $621,364

Therefore, the net cash flow in year 5 is the $62,569 flow generated from rent plus $621,364 from the net proceeds of the sale for a total of $683,933.

Now that our "T" bar is built, we can proceed, using our financial calculator, to determine the net present value, NPV of the discounted cash flows at 11% for the 5-year period, resulting in $192,346.

As presented in the previous sections, a positive NPV indicates that the internal rate of return, IRR of the investment will result higher than the one desired by the investor. In fact, if we calculate the IRR for this investment, it results in 22.58%, almost twice that desired.

Working with Sellers/Landlords

The services provided by Commercial Real Estate Consultants for sellers/landlords are diverse, and can include:

- Feasibility Analysis
- Obtaining Listing Assignments
- Negotiating
- Estimating Value
- Market Analysis
- Inspection ("Due Diligence")
- Relationships Landlord/Tenant
- Property Management

Feasibility Analysis:

A financial analysis of the property is crucial if we are to ascertain what the value of the property at market value is, should the owner want to sell, expand, or refinance the property. First, we need to get all the relevant data and fill in the "Annual Property Operational Data, or "APOD." From the APOD the projected financial analysis is performed; usually a 5-year projection.

Once the financial analysis model is built, it is possible to vary the different relevant parameters to perform a sensitivity analysis. For example, you can vary the leverage based on the initial investment, and analyze the different results obtained. Once the analysis is completed, the owner can choose which is the best option, depending on the value of money as related to other investment opportunities.

Obtaining Listings

Some commercial real estate advisors do not dare to tell their clients the truth about the price of a property, because they think they will lose the customer, and the client will end up handing the property to another sales advisor. These unscrupulous sales people capture the listing at a very high price with the conviction that the owner will decide to lower it in the future. The problem is not only to lower the price in about two or three months, the problem is that the property, as we say in commercial slang, burns and fails to attract an important part of the universe of buyers. We as commercial advisors must relay this to our clients, so they can understand the vicissitudes of the commercial real estate business.

Owners must be educated regarding the marketing of the property, as well as service and price. No matter how much marketing you do, if the price is not right, the marketing campaign, which costs money and effort, will be in vain.

There are different types of Listing Agreements:

- Exclusive Right to Sell the Property
- Exclusive Agency
- Open Listing
- Verbal Listing

Exclusive Right to Sell the Property:

This is the only type of contract that allows a commercial broker to secure his compensation if the property is sold, rent exchanged, or permuted. The exclusive right to sell/lease property states that the commercial broker is the exclusive agent, and that he will be compensated, regardless of who represents the buyer in the transaction. Many owners resist executing this type of contract, unless you and your firm have the credibility and a track record of success in selling or renting similar properties. It is very important to educate the owner and present facts that lead him to feel comfortable entering into an exclusivity agreement.

Exclusive Agency Listing:

This type of contract states that the commercial broker is the exclusive agent; however, the owner reserves the right to sell/lease the property to persons or entities with which the commercial broker has not had negotiations in the past, in which case, the owner is not responsible for compensating the broker.

It should be noted, that in this type of contract, the commercial broker and his firm can invest a significant amount of money and effort. If the owner sells/rent the property to a third party, all the resources invested will be down the drain, financially affecting the broker and the firm. In this type of situation, it is easy for other advisers to go behind your back, and do business directly with the owner, earning higher fees. Additionally, the Seller may market the property by himself in parallel with the marketing campaign the broker has implemented; this may cause lots of confusion in the market.

Open Listing:

This listing contract specifies in writing the price and the terms, but says that it can be canceled "At Will," offering no protection to the commercial broker, except for setting the terms and price. The owner can share this contract with other advisers at the same time, since none has exclusivity. Many owners offer this type of contract to advisers and/or signatories that do not know and are afraid to be tied to a consultant or agency for a significant period without knowing how they will perform.

Verbal Listing:

In this case, there is no contract "per se," only a verbal communication in which the owner communicates to the broker that if he procures a buyer for the property at a certain price, the owner will pay a commission. . It is very common in these cases for the owner to set a minimum price in this verbal agreement with the commercial broker. Whatever the broker gets above that price would be his compensation.

Of the types of contracts presented, the only acceptable one for a business relationship is the "Exclusive Authorization and the Right to Sell the Property." A professional broker should not accept any other type of contract.

Since commercial brokers generally work with sellers and buyers, in certain circumstances it is okay to accept work with an owner, laying down the conditions in a commission agreement, in case the broker procures a buyer.

As mentioned earlier, some owners do not feel comfortable providing exclusivity for the sale or lease, because they don't trust the commercial broker or its performance regarding the marketing of the property and all the activities promised, and they fear being limited by a contract that is not performing. To overcome this mistrust, the broker must present in the contract a detailed marketing plan, specifying each one of the activities to be carried out and compromise the execution by writing a clause that in the event that it fails to carry out any of the activities promised, the Broker will have an agreeable time to cure, otherwise the owner will be on its right to cancel the contract.

Obtaining a listing to sell commercial property requires a lot of preparation and knowledge; it is advisable to follow these steps:

1. Initial Investigation

The first step is to understand everything about the property and the owner: History, characteristics, specifications, neighborhood, etc.

2. Interview With the Owner:

This interview is crucial to gather all the relevant information on the property, take pictures, and find out why the owner wants to sell.

3. Estimate the Value:

Based on the information obtained, prepare an estimate of value by using the sales comparative approach and the income approach.

4. Preparation of the Document:

It is important to prepare a comprehensive listing presentation including an executive summary, an introduction, broker credentials, client's testimonials, the subject property specifications, the valuation already prepared, a marketing plan, and exhibits such as maps, pictures, demographics, and sales and lease comparables.

5. Conducting the Presentation:

Each Listing Presentation is a job interview. The consultant is asking for a job, the opportunity to list the commercial property for sale. If the steps above have been completed diligently, the consultant will have a thorough knowledge of the owner, the property and the market. This prior preparation before the final presentation makes the difference.

Below are several tips to keep in mind during the presentation:

1. Dress impeccably; presentation is always important

2. Be punctual; preferably arrive ten minutes before the appointment

3. Be sure that those who make decisions are present (this must be coordinated based on the information obtained in the investigation).

4. The presentation documents must contain all the relevant information and more! And these documents must be immaculately presented.

5. Emphasize the marketing plan and explain how this will bring results.

6. Highlight your company's database of investor/buyers/renters of the property

7. Indicate your availability and that of your team to show the property.

8. Go over all the activities in the marketing plan. The client will want to know the details of what you will do to rent or sell the property.

9. Present some examples of the marketing materials that will be used

10. Define with the owner the type and frequency of communications he will require for reporting on progress.

On some occasions, you will find objections in terms of:

Exclusivity: This objection is easy to overcome if you explain that each and every one of the activities of the marketing plan will be timely, and in the event that this does not happen, the consultant will have twenty-four hours to correct the problem, or the owner shall have the right to cancel the contract.

Very High Commissions: the objection to the commission is easy to refute, as it compensates for hard work, effort, and especially service provided. It should be emphasized that the objective is to sell/rent the property at fair market price in the minimum possible time.

Negotiation

Consultants must be able to negotiate for the benefit of his client. The negotiation process is an art that is achieved with experience and knowledge. A good knowledge of the property, market, and the handling of the financial concepts will make negotiation a smooth process.

Estimated Value:

As presented above, the estimation of value is crucial to conducting the business of commercial real estate. A commercial consultant must have the skills and knowledge to be able to evaluate a commercial property.

In contrast with a residential comparative market analysis, in estimating the value of commercial properties, two additional approaches to value must be considered. These three approaches to assessing the value of commercial properties are:

1. Sales Comparison Approach
2. Income Approach
3. Cost Reposition Approach

Market Analysis:

The owner should, at all times, be familiar with the property and the current values of the market. For instance, what kind of concessions, are being offered in the market? Have there been changes in demography? What new projects are being developed? As the owner's consultant, you should continually monitor the internal and external variables, and be able to anticipate market situations and avoid pitfalls by advising on the corresponding decisions.

Inspection ("Due Diligence")

The inspection process or "Due Diligence" is crucial to the successful completion of a commercial transaction. The consultant should advise the owner on all activities, documentation, support, and to be prepared when the potential buyer begins to review the different aspects of the property. The consultant should prepare a package with the most recent surveys and environmental studies, leases, contracts, detailed operating expenses, the last three years P&L's and Income Tax, any improvements or construction performed along with the corresponding permits (open & closed), as well as other documents.

Landlord/Tenant Relationships

Independent of state and local regulations, understanding the landlord/tenant relationship is essential for the proper development of the business. The consultant must represent the landlord by ensuring his interests and enforcing contracts and established standards and procedures. It is of the utmost importance to establish an excellent relationship with the tenants, providing support and assisting them in their needs.

Property Management

An activity that commercial real estate consultants can provide, is property management of commercial properties. In this field, commercial consultants must have the knowledge, the appropriate infrastructure, and the necessary tools to effectively administrate the property. This provides several advantages in the business:

1. Constant Cash Flow
2. Control of the Property
3. Signs in the Property
4. Economies of Scale

Working with Buyers/Tenants

Commercial customers tend to analyze a series of details such as site selection, buy/lease analysis, investment opportunity, and regulations.

The services provided by Commercial Real Estate Consultants for buyers/tenants are diverse, and can include:

- Feasibility Analysis
- Search and Selection of Properties
- Estimation of Value
- Valuation of Income
- Purchase/Lease Analysis
- Negotiation
- Inspection Process "Due Diligence"
- Property Management

Feasibility Analysis:

Financial analysis of the property is crucial to ascertain its value on the market and to be able to compare it with other investment opportunities based on the desired rate of return. First, we need to get all the relevant data and fill it in the form of "Annual Property Operational Data, or "APOD." From the APOD, the projected financial analysis is performed; this is usually a 5-year projection.

Once the financial analysis model is built, it is possible to vary the different relevant parameters to perform a sensitivity analysis. For example, you can vary the leverage based on the initial investment, and analyze the different results obtained. The completed analysis allows the investor to choose the best option depending on the value of money as related to other investment opportunities.

Search and Selection of Properties:

The commercial real estate consultant must understand very clearly what the requirements of the buyer or tenant are. In the case of the buyer, is this an investor or an end user? What are his expectations of return? How much is the cost of money for his business operation?

Once the search parameters are established, the commercial consultant must assemble a long list of about 6 to 8 properties (depending on the market), study them comparatively and visit them to verify conditions, access, neighborhoods, driving times, amenities, restrictions, etc.

After having a clear understanding of the different options, the commercial consultant must meet the buyer or tenant and review this long list. The client will select those properties he likes, and usually the long list gets reduced to 3 to 4 properties and is called the short list. The consultant proceeds to prepare a tour to take the client to see the properties on the short list. Depending on the results of the tour, the consultant then prepares an in-depth analysis of the properties to present to and discuss with the client.

Estimated Value:

The market value represents the most important information for making a decision regarding investment and proceeding to write an offer. A commercial consultant must have the skills and knowledge to be able to evaluate a commercial property. In contrast to a residential comparative market analysis, in estimating the value of commercial properties, two additional approaches must be considered. The Cost reposition Approach and the Income Approach as presented in section 4 of this book:

     1. Sales Comparison Approach
     2. Cost Reposition Approach
     3. Income Approach

Market Analysis:

The investor should be familiar with the market in which he will be investing, the types of properties and the leverage or financing available in that particular market. The consultant should educate the client and provide him with market conditions such as cap rates, changes in demography, new projects being developed, etc. The consultant must help the investor feel comfortable by mitigating the risks involved in the selection of the specific property.

Purchase/Lease Analysis

If an end user is uncertain about buying or renting, the commercial consultant should present a financial study based on the cost of money, comparing the option of acquiring vs. the option to rent. Even though the financial decision is important, other variables apply, such as exposure, location, establishment of the point of trade, etc.

Negotiation

Consultants must be able to negotiate for the benefit of his client. The negotiation process is an art that is achieved with experience and knowledge. A good knowledge of the property, market, and the handling of the financial concepts will make negotiation a smooth process.

Inspection Process "Due Diligence"

When representing the buyer/tenant, the commercial counselor must become a "maestro," the conductor of the orchestra, leading the team that will be recruited to perform the different tasks involved in the process of due diligence. There are four fields of action in the due diligence:

1. **Legal:**

Performed by an attorney specializing in Commercial Real Estate

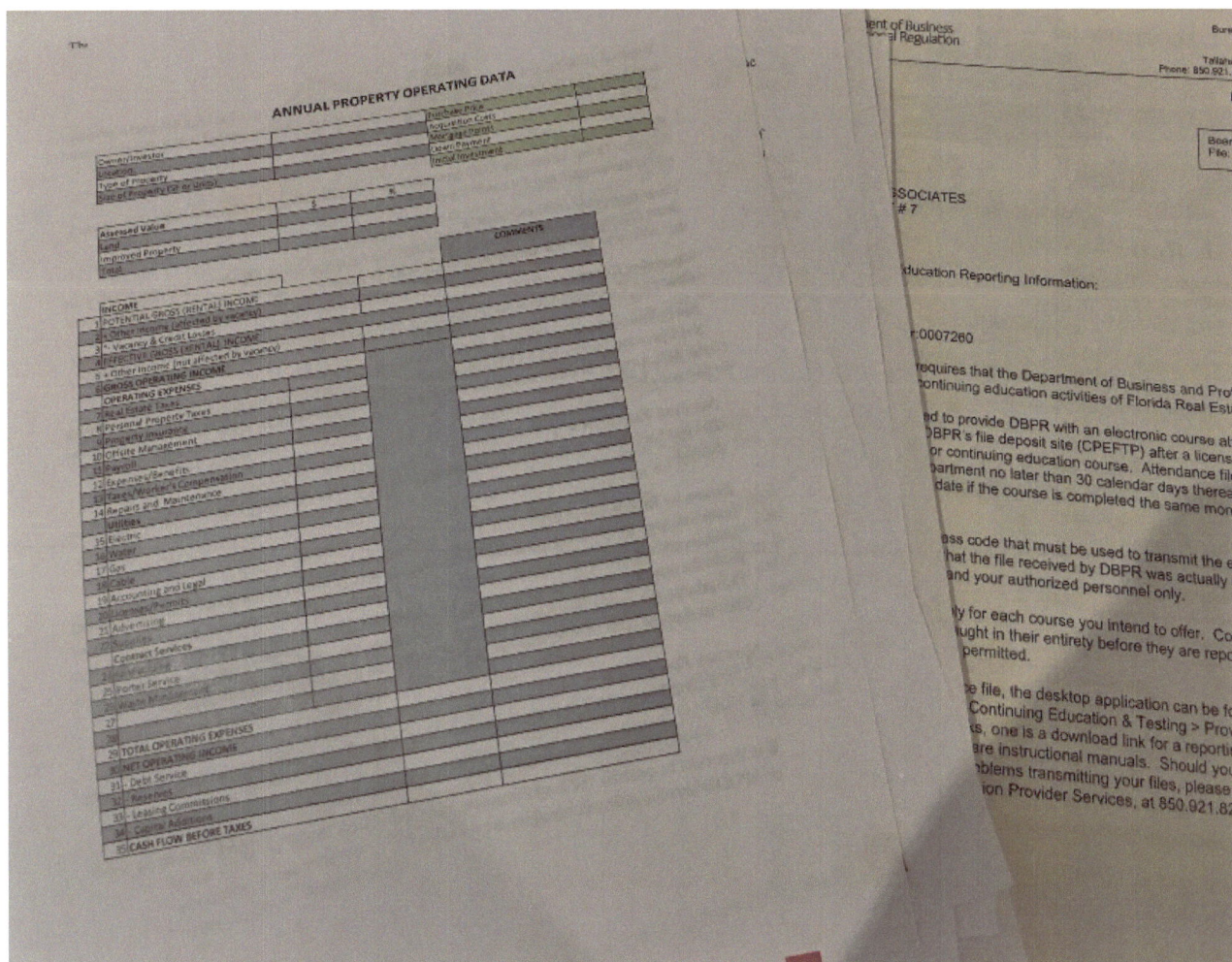

yapi group

Construction • Engineering • Inspections • Project Management • Environmental • Indoor Air Quality

COMMERCIAL PROPERTY INSPECTION PROPOSAL

In Regards To	2185-2189 North State Road-7, Margate, FL 33063		
Prepared For	J.M. Padron	Date of Proposal	November 16, 2016
Type of Facility	8,243 SQ. FT. • <1 Acres Lot	Folio Number	4841-25-08-0316

CODE	ASSIGNMENT	FEE
C-CASBA	❖ Commercial Auto Shop Building Assessment *Eligible for 25% of Exclusive YAPI Discount & will remain effective for 35 days*	$ 2,245.00
	TOTAL AMOUNT OF PROPOSED INSPECTION FEE	**$ 1,570.00**

SCOPE OF THE INSPECTION & THE AGREEMENT

The inspection would include a visual, non-invasive of readily accessible areas. This is a non-destructive inspection and it would not be technically exhaustive and no excavation, disassembly or removal of obstructions is performed. The Standards of Practice meet those prescribed by the American Society for Testing and Materials, ASTM Designation E 2018-15 and FS.718.606.

The property inspection will consist of inspecting structural, roof, foundation, and electrical, mechanical, HVAC and plumbing systems for the subject property. The systems and the structure will be inspected to determine the condition and the working status. Digital photos will be taken and provided in the report of major items along with photos of all found marginal or defective items.

Access will be required to all offices, attic areas, mechanical rooms, storage areas and any other areas that are normally locked or not accessible for safety or security. The client understands, accepts and agrees that YAPI Group will not impliedly or expressly warrant or guarantee the condition of the subject properties and the deficiencies. Damages for any claimed deficiency in the inspection of the subject property to discover a claimed defect shall be limited to the fee charged for the inspection.

YAPI Group will not express any opinion on the condition of this property beyond what will be set forth in the written report. YAPI Group does not check for compliance with building codes or regulations of any federal, state or local governmental body, entity or agency. The client, or company representative by his/her signature below, accepts and understands all of the terms of this Agreement and that the total proposed inspection fee is due upon delivery of the completed inspection report.

Respectfully Submitted,

[signature]

Omer Zeyrek, PhD
CGC, PMP, CPI, CMA, CMR, RMES, RMIS
State of FL Licensed Inspector • Lic. #003932

Client Name & Signature – Date

8306 MILLS DR • 130 • MIAMI FL 33183
(305) 760-YAPI • (305) 600-0090 • (855) YAPI INC
YapiGroup.com

2. Engineering (structural, electrical, mechanical):

Made by an Engineering Inspection Company

LANDSCIENCE
Environmental Consultants and Engineers

December 02, 2016

Mr. Lawrence McGill

Subject: Phase II Environmental Site Assessment Screening Update Report for the
Auto Body Shop Property
Located at 2187 North State Road 7
Margate, Broward County, FL
LandScience Project Number: 2166968

Dear Mr. McGill,

LandScience is pleased to submit the attached report on a Phase II Environmental Site Assessment (ESA) for the above referenced property. The Phase II ESA was conducted in general accordance with good commercial and customary practices with respect to the range of contaminants within the scope of the Comprehensive Environmental Response, Compensation, and Liability Act (i.e., Superfund) and petroleum products, as described in the American Society for Testing and Materials document Standard Practice for Environmental Site Assessments: Phase II Environmental Site Assessment Process (ASTM E 1903-11).

LandScience appreciates the opportunity to assist you on this project. We look forward to providing you with our services again in the near future. Please feel free to contact us if you have questions concerning the report.

Yours Very Truly,

LandScience, Inc.

[signature]

Andrew Whitaker
Project Manager

[signature]

Rob Ludicke, M.Sc., REP # 5985
President

3. Environmental:

Made by a company of Environmental Engineering.

12570 NE 7th Ave, North Miami, Florida 33161   Tel 305.893.4955 Fax 305.893.9364

4. Accounting:

Carried out by an experienced Accountant.

5. Marketing

Usually performed by the Commercial Consultant

6. Financial Analysis

Usually performed by the Commercial Consultant

N	$		Net Flow less Debt Service		Net Flow end of the period	
0	$	(375,000)	$	(375,000)	$	(375,000)
1	$	165,000	$	51,708	$	51,708
2	$	160,938	$	47,646	$	47,646
3	$	165,766	$	52,474	$	52,474
4	$	170,739	$	57,447	$	57,447
5	$	175,861	$	62,569	$	683,933
Net Present Value						$192,346

Each part of the inspection must be carried out in detail, so the consultant can combine the results of each in a comprehensive report of acceptance, acceptance with conditions, or rejection.

Property Management

An activity that commercial real estate consultants can provide, is property management of commercial properties. In this field, commercial consultants must have the knowledge, the appropriate infrastructure, and the necessary tools to effectively administrate the property.

Property Management is an excellent opportunity if the investor is absentee or just doesn't want to get involved in the management of the property. The administration of properties represents several advantages in the business:

1. Constant Cash Flow
2. Control of the Property
3. Signs in the Property
4. Economies of Scale

Some of the activities or tasks provided by a commercial consultant may not be related to the purchase-sale or commercial lease, but they can be consulting activities. To mention some: preparing a valuation for the purpose of refinancing or for a property tax appeal; coordinating due diligence; negotiating an existing lease, etc. The compensation for these activities is usually by the hour. How much? It depends on the commercial consultant's hourly value.

Case of Study

A community type shopping center generates the following net operating income stream:

N	$
0	
1	850,000.00
2	884,000.00
3	919,360.00
4	956,134.40
5	994,379.78

The property has been placed in the market with an asking price of $14 million.

The investor went to a local bank to find out about the terms and conditions to get a loan for the purchase. The bank officer told him that the bank could finance up to 70% of the purchase price at an interest rate of 5.25% for a term of ten (10) years with an amortization of 25 years.

It is estimated, based on market conditions that the property could be sold in five years at a capitalization rate of 6.5 %. Sales commission is estimated at 5%of the sale price.

The investor is analyzing similar opportunities with a performance of 7% yield.

Part 1. Calculate the Net Present Value and the IRR of this investment.

Approach:

Step 1. Mortgage Calculation

Term	10 Years
Interest Rate	5.25%
Amortization	25 Years
LTV	70%
Selling Price	$ 14,000,000
Mortgage Amount	$ 9,800,000
Initial Investment	($ 4,200,000)
Monthly Payment	$ 58,726
Annual Payment, Debt Service	$ 704,715

Step 2. Projected Sales at the end of the Period.

Capitalization Rate	6.5%
NOI at the end of the year	$ 994,380
Projected Value of Sale	$ 15,298,154

Step 3. Balance of the Mortgage at the end of the Period.

Mortgage Amortization	60 Months
Principal	$ 240,284
Interest	$ 464,431
Balance	$ 8,715,112

Step 4. Net Flow at the end of the Period.

Sale Price	$ 15,298,150
Less payment of the Mortgage Balance	$ 8,715,112
Sales Commission	$764,908
Total Net Sales Proceeds	$ 5,818,120

Step 5. Calculation of the Net Present Value

N	NOI	Debt Service	Cash Flow	Sales Proceeds	Net Cash Flows
0					$ (4,200,000)
1	$ 850,000	$ (704,715)	$145,285		$ 145,285
2	$ 884,000	$ (704,715)	$179,285		$ 179,285
3	$ 919,360	$ (704,715)	$214,645		$ 214,645
4	$ 956,134	$ (704,715)	$251,419		$ 251,419
5	$ 994,380	$ (704,715)	$289,665	$ 5,818,120	$ 6,107,785
			NPV @	**7%**	**$ 814,162**

IRR	**11.13%**

The net present value is $814,162 positive, which means that the investor will receive a better return than his desired rate of 7%. The IRR results in 11.13% which indeed is greater than the yield desired by the investor.

Part 2. If in addition to the financing terms above, the bank sets a DSCR of 1.25, what would be the purchase price that you would advise to write the offer for?

Step 1. Calculation of the New Mortgage

With the debt service ratio of 1.25 and the NOI of the first year of $850,000, we can calculate the Debt Service as:

DS = NOI/DSCR = $850,000/1.25 = $680,000 and the monthly payments will be $56,667

Term	10 Years
Interest Rate	5.25%
Amortization	25 Years
PMT	($56,667)
Amount of New Mortgage	$9,456,356
LTV	70%

Step 2. Calculation of the new purchase price.

If the new mortgage is $9,456,356, the new value of the property would be:

$9,456,356/70% = $13,509,080.

The Investor has two options:

1. Try it to negotiate a price reduction from $14,000,000 to $13,509,080, or;
2. Increase his initial investment from $4,200,000 to $4,690,920

Scenario 1. Seller accepts reduction in price

Step 1. Mortgage Calculation

Term	10 Years
Interest Rate	5.25%
Amortization	25 Years
LTV	70%
Selling Price	$ 13,509,080
Mortgage Amount	$ 9,456,356
Initial Investment	($ 4,052,724)
Monthly Payment	$ 56,667
Annual Payment, Debt Service	$ 680,004

Step 2. Projected Sales at the end of the Period.

Capitalization Rate	6.5%
NOI at the end of the year	$ 994,380
Projected Value of Sale	$ 15,298,154

Step 3. Balance of the Mortgage at the end of the Period.

Mortgage Amortization	60 Months
Balance EOY 5	$ 8,409,266

Step 4. Net Flow at the end of the Period.

Sale Price	$ 15,298,150
Less payment of the Mortgage Balance	$ 8,409,266
Sales Commission	$764,908
Total Net Sales Proceeds	$ 6,123,976

Step 5. Calculation of the Net Present Value

N	NOI	Debt Service	Cash Flow	Sales Proceeds	Net Cash Flows
0					$ (4,052,724)
1	$ 850,000	$ (680,004)	$ 169,996		$ 169,996
2	$ 884,000	$ (680,004)	$ 203,996		$ 203,996
3	$ 919,360	$ (680,004)	$ 239,356		$ 239,356
4	$ 956,134	$ (680,004)	$ 276,130		$ 276,130
5	$ 994,380	$ (680,004)	$ 314,376	$ 6,123,976	$ 6,438,352
			NPV @	**7%**	**$ 1,280,829**

IRR	**13.52%**

The net present value is $1,280,829 positive, which means that the investor will receive a better return than his desired rate of 7%.

In fact the IRR results in 13.52% which is higher than in the previous calculation.

Scenario 2. Investor increases the initial investment

Step 1. Mortgage Calculation

Term	10 Years
Interest Rate	5.25%
Amortization	25 Years
LTV	70%
Selling Price	$ 13,509,080
Mortgage Amount	$ 9,456,356
Initial Investment	($ 4,690,920)
Monthly Payment	$ 56,667
Annual Payment, Debt Service	$ 680,004

Step 2. Projected Sales at the end of the Period.

Capitalization Rate	6.5%
NOI at the end of the year	$ 994,380
Projected Value of Sale	$ 15,298,154

Step 3. Balance of the Mortgage at the end of the Period.

Mortgage Amortization	60 Months
Balance EOY 5	$ 8,409,266

Step 4. Net Flow at the end of the Period.

Sale Price	$ 15,298,150
Less payment of the Mortgage Balance	$ 8,409,266
Sales Commission	$764,908
Total Net Sales Proceeds	$ 6,123,976

Step 5. Calculation of the Net Present Value

N	NOI	Debt Service	Cash Flow	Sales Proceeds	Net Cash Flows
0					$ (4,690,920)
1	$ 850,000	$ (680,004)	$ 169,996		$ 169,996
2	$ 884,000	$ (680,004)	$ 203,996		$ 203,996
3	$ 919,360	$ (680,004)	$ 239,356		$ 239,356
4	$ 956,134	$ (680,004)	$ 276,130		$ 276,130
5	$ 994,380	$ (680,004)	$ 314,376	$ 6,123,976	$ 6,438,352
			NPV @	**7%**	**$ 642,633**

IRR	**9.99%**

The net present value is $642,633 positive, which means that the investor will receive a better return than his desired rate of 7%.

This IRR results, as expected, in a lower value that in the two previous calculations.

Glossary

A

Agent
An individual/entity who transacts, represents, or manages business for another individual/entity. Permission is provided by the individual/entity being represented.

APOD
Annual Property Operating Data

Assignee
Individual to whom a contract is assigned.

Assignment
The manner by which a contract is transferred from one individual to another individual.

Assignor
An individual who transfers a contract to another individual

B

BOMA
Building Owners and Managers Association

Build Out
The construction or improvements of the interior of a space, including flooring, walls, finished plumbing, electrical work, etc.

Building Permit
Written government permission to develop, renovate, or repair a building.

C

Cancellation Clause
A provision in a contract (e.g., lease) that confers the ability of one in the lease to terminate the party's obligations. The grounds and ability to cancel are usually specified in the lease.

Capital Improvement

Any major physical development or redevelopment to a property that extends the life of the property. Examples include upgrading the elevators, replacement of the roof, and renovations of the lobby.

Capitalization Rate (Cap Rate)

The value given to the property when the Net Operating Income (NOI) is divided by the current market value or sales price. A cap rate can be used as a rough indicator of how quickly an investment will pay for itself.

Certificate of Occupancy (CO)

The government issues this official form, which states that the building is legally ready to be occupied.

Chattel

Household goods, including personal property such as lamps, desks, and chairs.

Common Area Maintenance (CAM)

This is the amount of additional rent charged to the tenant, in addition to the base rent, to maintain the common areas of the property shared by the tenants and from which all tenants benefit. Examples include: snow removal, outdoor lighting, parking lot sweeping, escalators, sidewalks, skyways, parking areas. Most often, this does not include any capital improvements that are made to the property.

Commission Split

An agreed upon division of commissions earned between a sales agent and sponsoring broker, or between the selling broker and listing broker

Contiguous

Touching at some point or along a boundary

Contingency

A requirement in a contract that must occur before that contract can be finalized

Contract

A legal agreement between entities that requires each to conduct (or refrain from conducting) certain activities. This document provides each party with a right that is enforceable under our judicial system.

Covenants

Wording found in deeds that limits/restricts the use to which a property may be put (e.g., no bars).
Back to top

D

Deed

A signed, written instrument that conveys title to real property.

Deed Restriction

An imposed restriction in a deed that limits the use of the property. For example, a restriction could prohibit the sale of alcoholic beverages.

Default

Failure to fulfill a promise, discharge an obligation, or perform certain acts.

Delivery

Transfer something from one entity to another.

E

Eminent Domain

The government's right to condemn and acquire property for public use. The government must provide the owner fair compensation.

Endorsement

Signing one's name on the back of a check.

Escrow

A written agreement among parties requiring, that certain property/funds be placed with a third party. The object in escrow is released to a designated entity upon completion of some specific occurrence.

Estoppel Certificate

A legal instrument executed by the one taking out the mortgage (i.e., mortgagor). The owner of a property may require an individual leasing a property to sign an estoppel certificate, which verifies the major points (e.g., base rent, lease commencement and expiration) existing lease between the landlord and tenant.

Eviction (Actual)

Physical removal of a tenant either by law or force.

Eviction (Proceeding)

A legal proceeding by the landlord to remove a tenant

Exclusive Agency
An agreement in which one broker has exclusive rights to represent the owner or tenant. If another broker is used, both the original and actual broker are entitled to leasing commissions.

F

Full Service Lease
A lease of property whereby the landlord (i.e., lessor) pays for all property charges usually included in ownership. These charges can include insurance, taxes, utilities, janitorial and maintenance, among others.

Fiduciary
A person who represents another on financial/property matters.

Fixtures
Personal property so attached the land or building (e.g., improvements) it is considered part of the real property.

G

Grace Period
Additional time allowed to complete an action (e.g., make a payment) before a default or violation occurs.

Gross Potential Income
The maximum income a property may generate by rents.

Gross Income
The Total Income Generated by Rents

Gross Effective Income
The total income generated by rent plus any additional income

Gross Lease
A lease of property whereby the landlord (i.e., lessor) pays for all property charges usually included in ownership. These charges can include insurance, utilities, taxes, and maintenance, among others.

H

Hard Money Loan
An asset-based loan in which a borrower receives funds that are secured by the value of a piece of real estate and often at a higher interest rate than a traditional commercial property loan. They are used for acquisitions, turnaround situations, foreclosures and bankruptcies.

Highest and Best Use
The optimum use a property has based on the zoning ordinances, the physical capability and the financial feasibility.

Holdover Tenant
A tenant who remains in possession of leased property after the lease term expiration.

I

Incompetent
An individual who is unable to handle his own affairs by reason of some medical condition (e.g., insanity, Alzheimer's).

Instrument
A written legal document created to secure the rights of the parties participating in the agreement. Irrevocable, Incapable of being altered, changed, or recalled.

J

Joint Tenancy
Ownership of real property by two or more individuals, each of whom has an undivided interest with the right of survivorship.

Judgment
A formal decision issued by a court relating to the specific claims and rights of the parties to an act or suit.

L

Landlord
One who rents property to a tenant.

Lease
A contract whereby the landlord grants the tenant the right to occupy defined space for a set period at a specific price (i.e., rent).

Leasehold
The estate or interest a tenant has as stated in the tenant's lease.

Lessee
An individual (i.e., tenant) to whom property is rented under a lease.

Lessor

An individual (i.e. landlord) who rents property to a tenant via a lease.

Letter of Intent

A document, usually non-binding, agreement among parties indicating their serious desire to move forward with negotiations.

Listing

An employment contract between principal and agent that authorizes the agent (such as a broker) to perform services for the principal and his property.

Loss Factor

What percentage of the gross area of a space is lost due to walls, elevator, etc. Rule of thumb in Manhattan is approximately 15%

M

Mandatory

A requirement that must be conformed to as specified in any written document.

Market Price

The actual selling or leasing price of a property.

Market Value

The expected price that a property should bring if exposed for lease in the open market for a reasonable period of time and with market savvy landlords and tenants.

Meeting of the Minds

When all individuals to a contract agree to the substance and terms of that contract.

Minor

A person under a legal age, usually under 18 years old.

N

Net Lease

Also called triple net lease. The lessee pays not only a fixed rental charge but also expenses on the rented property, including maintenance.

NOI

Net Operating Income, it is the net income at the end of the year, Gross Effective Income minus the Operating Expenses.

Non-Disturbance Agreement

The tenant signs this to prevent himself from being evicted if the property owner does not pay its mortgage to the bank.

O

Obligee

The person who will receive the outcome of an obligation.

Obligor

An individual who has engaged to perform an obligation to another person (i.e., obligee).

Open Listing

A listing given to any broker without liability to compensate any broker except the one who first secures a buyer who is ready, willing, and able to meet the terms of the listing, or secures the acceptance by the landlord of a satisfactory offer; the lease of the property automatically terminates the listing.

Operating Expense

All the expenses incurred for the operation of the property: property taxes, insurance and maintenance.

Option

A right given to purchase or lease a property upon specified terms within a specified time. If the right is not exercised, the option holder is not subject to liability for damages. If the holder of the option exercises it, the grantor of option must perform the option's requirements.

P

Percentage Lease

A lease of property in which the rent is based upon the percentage of the sales volume made on the specific premises. There is usually a clause for a minimum rent as well.

Personal Property

Any property which is not real property. Examples include furniture, clothing, and artwork.

Power of Attorney

A written instrument duly signed and executed by an individual which authorizes an agent to act on his behalf to the extent indicated in the document.

Principal

The employer (e.g., landlord) of an agent or broker. This is the agent's or broker's client.

Q

Quiet Enjoyment

The right of a landlord or tenant to use the property without disturbances.

R

Real Estate Board

An organization whose members consist primarily of real estate professionals such as brokers.

Real Estate Syndicate

When partners (either with or without unlimited liability) form a partnership to participate in a real estate venture.

Real Property

Land and any capital improvements (e.g., buildings) erected on the property.

Realtor

A coined word which may only be used by an active member of a local real estate board, affiliated with the National Association of Real Estate Boards.

Rent

Compensation from tenant to landlord for the use of real estate.

Restriction

A restriction, often specified in the deed, on the use of property.

Revocation

An act of rescinding power previously authorized.

Rule of Thumb

A common or ubiquitous benchmark. For example, it is often assumed that each worker in an office will need approximately 250 square feet of space. Back to top

S

Situs

The location of a property.

Specific Performance

When a court requires a defendant to carry out the terms of an agreement or contract.

Square Feet

The usual method by which rental space is defined. It is the area of that space, calculated by taking length times width. For example, a room 30 feet by 60 feet has an area of 1,800 square feet.

Statute

A law established by an act of legislature.

Statute of Frauds

State law (founded on ancient English law) which requires that contracts must be reduced to written form if it is to be enforced by law.

Statute of Limitations

A law barring all right of redress after a certain period of time from the moment when a cause of action first arises.

Subagent

An agent of an individual already acting as an agent of a principal.

Subleasing

The leasing of space from one tenant to another tenant.

Subscribing Witness

The witness to the execution of an instrument who has written his name as proof of seeing such execution.

Surrender

The cancellation of a lease by mutual consent of the tenant and the landlord.

T

Tenancy at Will

A license to occupy or use lands and buildings at the will of the landlord.

Tenancy by the Entirety
An estate which exists only between husband and wife. Each has equal right of enjoyment and possession during their joint lives, and each has the right of survivorship.

Tenant Improvements
Work done on the interior of a space, can be paid for by landlord, tenant, or some combination of both, depending on the terms of the lease.

Tenancy in Common
Ownership of property by two or more individuals, each of whom has an undivided interest, without the right of survivorship.

Tenants at Sufferance
An individual who comes to possess land via lawful title and keeps it in perpetuity without any title.

Tie-in Arrangement
A contract where one transaction depends upon another transaction.

Triple Net Lease
A lease requiring tenants to pay all utilities, insurance, taxes, and maintenance costs. Back to top

U

Urban Property
Property in a city or a high-density area.

V

Valid
A binding situation that is authorized and enforceable by law.

Valuation
Estimated price, value, or worth. Also, the act of identifying a property's worth via an appraisal.

Variance
Government authorization to use or develop a property in a manner which is not permitted by the applicable zoning regulations.

Violation
Act, condition, or deed that violates the permissible use of property.

Void
Something that is unenforceable.

Voidable
A situation which is capable of being unenforceable but is not so unless direct action is taken.

W

Waiver
The intentional relinquishment or abandonment of a specific claim, privilege, or right.

Work Letter
An amount of money that a landlord agrees to spend on the construction of the interior of a space per, the lease, usually negotiated.

Back to top

Z

Zone
An area, delineated by a governmental authority, which is authorized for and limited to specific uses.

Zoning Ordinance
A law by a local governmental authority (e.g., city or county) that sets the parameters for which the property may be put to use.

References

1. Fundamentals of Commercial Real Estate by JM Padron.

2. Foundations for Success in Commercial Real Estate – The CCIM Institute's Robert L. Ward Center for Real Estate.

3. International Council of Shopping Centers, ICSC.

4. CCIM Institute

Answers to selected Exercises

Example 3.1

IOB = $60,000
N0I = $52,000
DS = $27,600
NCF = $24,400
II = $150,000
ROI = 16.27%

Example 3.2

PGI = $144,000
Vacancy = $18,000
EGI = $126,000
GOI = $126,000
NOI = $82,800
NCF = $82,800
II = VALUE = $920,000

Example 3.3

Scenario 1
NOI = $35,000
NCF = $35,000
ROI = 7%

Scenario 2

Property 1
NCF = $18,604
ROI = 7.44%

Property 2
NCF = $23,604
ROI = 9.44%

The Combined
NCF = $42,208
ROI = 8.42%

The investor would obtain a better ROI in Scenario 2, and it would get even better with time as the two properties are being amortized.

Example 4.3

Sale Price Warehouse   = $800,000
Sale Price Retail   = $800,000
Total Proceeds   = $1,600,000

Shopping Center Value = $2,000,000

John is short $400,000 to buy the shopping center upon the sale of his two propetrties. Then he can proceed as follows:

Option 1
Negotiate a private mortgage with the Seller for two years, endorsing the leases as a guarantee.

Option 2
Ask for a loan for 2 years to a financial institution.

Option 3
Ask for a loan for 10 years with an amortization at 20 years, to better leverage his investment.

Example 4.4

Taking the average of the net rents/sf/year and discarding the comps out of range, the result is:

$32.56/SF/year which represents the NOI per SF

Doing the same with the sales price, the result is:

$447.09/SF/year which represents the value per SF.

Applying the formula of the CAP rate, the result is 7.28%